THE LIVING FLAME

★

'He shall baptize you with the Holy Ghost and with fire.'
JOHN THE BAPTIST

'I came to cast fire upon the earth.'

'Ye shall receive power when the Holy Ghost is come upon you.'
JESUS TO HIS DISCIPLES

TO A
MOTHER AND FATHER
WHO POSSESS THE LIVING FLAME

THE LIVING FLAME

Being a study of The Gift of the Spirit
in the New Testament

WITH SPECIAL REFERENCE TO
PROPHECY, GLOSSOLALIA, MONTANISM
AND PERFECTION

MAURICE BARNETT
M.A., B.D.

WIPF & STOCK · Eugene, Oregon

Wipf and Stock Publishers
199 W 8th Ave, Suite 3
Eugene, OR 97401

The Living Flame
Being a Study of the Gifts of the Spirit in the New Testament With Special Reference to Prophecy, Glossolalia, Montanism, and Perfection
By Barnett, Maurice
Copyright©1953 Methodist Publishing - Epworth Press
ISBN 13: 978-1-4982-0503-0
Publication date 9/11/2014
Previously published by Epworth Press, 1953

Every effort has been made to trace the current copyright owner of this publication but without success. If you have any information or interest in the copyright, please contact the publishers.

Foreword

ONE OF THE pleasing compensations available to a senescent professor is that of seeing the varied achievements of his former students; and the pleasure is particularly keen when it is a contribution to his own subject that is to be welcomed and commended to the reader.

Mr Barnett began to study the subject to which the present work is devoted a good many years ago, as an academic exercise. Since then his energies have been given in part to academic work, but much more to the day-to-day tasks of an active ministry in the heart of a large industrial community. What appears in this book is thus the result both of serious study of the biblical material and the relevant literature (as is evidenced by the bibliography), and of wide experience in the working life of the Church. There is no part of Christian doctrine where this combination of study and practice is more important and necessary for a right understanding of the truth by which we live. For the Holy Spirit is far more than a topic for historical research or theological speculation; He is the continuing life and power of the Church, now no less than in the Apostolic Age.

I believe that what Mr Barnett here offers out of his studies and his ministerial experience will prove illuminating and encouraging to other students and ministers of the Word; and I hope that many more will prove it so.

MANCHESTER
August 1953

T. W. MANSON

Preface

THE following pages come from the conflict of the battlefield. This is not offered as an excuse for any deficiencies occasioned by the hurry of an active ministry, but rather as a cause impelling the study.

In a world seemingly held by sinister demonic forces, those engaged in the task of 'offering Christ' are often haunted by a crippling sense of weakness. Confronted by pagan ideologies or deadening apathy the Christian seems to make little decisive impact upon society. On the other hand, a perusal of the early documents of the Christian faith introduces a man into an atmosphere of power and life, deep certainty and infectious hope. Men were aflame as we are not aflame.

In the thrust and heat of the battlefield, surrounded by the clamouring demands of needy men, I went back to the documents of the primitive Church. That retreat was no withdrawal in face of enemy forces, it was rather to discover adequate resources for engaging the enemy, and to remind myself that the Power of the Spirit was still available to make us 'more than conquerors'.

These pages offer no originality, save that materials already available are brought together in my own way. Indebtedness to many teachers and writers is apparent from references. But one's debt to unknown folk who, as they have walked 'the Way' have unconsciously given evidence in life of their possession of the Spirit, can never be expressed.

Every attempt to trace 'sources' has been made, and grateful thanks are offered to the following Publishing Houses and authors for permission to use quotations: The Clarendon Press, Oxford, *The Idea of Perfection* by R. Newton Flew; James Clarke & Co. Ltd., *The Fellowship of the Spirit* by C. A. Scott; T. & T. Clark, *The Religious Experience of the Primitive Church* by P. G. S. Hopwood; Duckworth & Co. Ltd., *The Religious Ideas of the Old Testament* by H. Wheeler Robinson; Hodder & Stoughton Ltd., *Prophecy and Divination* by A. Guillaume, *A Faith to Proclaim* by J. S. Stewart, *The Spirit in the New Testament* by E. F. Scott, and *The Indwelling Spirit* by E. W. Davidson; Macmillan & Co. Ltd., *The Beginnings of Christianity* by

Foakes Jackson and Kirsopp Lake, *Studies in Mystical Religion* by Rufus Jones; Manchester University Press, *St Paul in Ephesus* by T. W. Manson; James Nisbet & Co. Ltd., *Redemption and Revelation* by H. Wheeler Robinson; and University Press, Cambridge, *The Teaching of Jesus* by T. W. Manson. If any due acknowledgement has been omitted, or copyright infringed, I trust I may be forgiven for such seeming discourtesy.

My former teacher, the Rev. Dr T. W. Manson, Rylands Professor in Biblical Criticism and Exegesis in the University of Manchester, has constantly given encouragement. I am grateful to my friend, the Rev. Dr Norman H. Snaith, M.A., of Headingley College, Leeds, who has read through the proofs and was, as ever, most helpful with suggestions.

A former colleague, Sister Edith Walton, who, despite the heavy tasks of pastoral responsibility that fall to the lot of a Methodist Deaconess, with infinite patience prepared the manuscript for the Press. My present colleagues, the Rev. Francis N. Jasper, and Miss Eileen Stockdill, with skill and willingness, helped to remove defects from the proofs and compiled the Index. The Rev. Frank Cumbers and his colleagues of the Epworth Press are never without grace or courtesy.

Finally, I must record my ever-increasing debt to the fellowship of the Church in which I have been called to serve. The People called Methodists have taught me more of the 'Fellowship of the Spirit' than ever could be read in most excellent books.

In a situation where the opposing evil forces are ruthless and passionate, Christian warriors must not yield to lukewarmness, but be aflame with the Spirit. If the following pages help someone to think again about the experience of 'the gift of the Spirit' which brings abounding vitality, missionary passion, and conquering love; if they are reminded that there are powerful and adequate resources for our warfare—a fervent prayer will have been answered.

Maurice Barnett

EASTBROOK HALL,
BRADFORD
August, 1953

Contents

FOREWORD	. . . .	v
PREFACE	. . . .	vii
ABSTRACT OF THE STUDY	. . . . .	xi
INTRODUCTION: THE SUBJECT AND METHOD OF THE STUDY	. . . .	xv

Section One—Abnormal and Supernormal Phenomena in the Religious Life of the Old and New Testaments

1	DREAM FANTASIES	. . . . . .	3
2	PROPHECY	. . . .	11
3	GLOSSOLALIA	. . . .	27

Section Two—The Contemporary Explanation of Abnormal and Supernormal Phenomena

4	THE SPIRIT-CONSCIOUS PEOPLE	. . . .	35
5	SPIRIT IN HEBREW PSYCHOLOGY	. . . .	38
6	THE EXPERIENCE OF THE SPIRIT	. . . .	43
7	THE EXPERIENCE OF SPIRIT- AND DEMON-POSSESSION	. . . .	70

Section Three—Significance of the Abnormal and Supernormal Phenomena in relation to certain New Testament and Early Church Problems

8	THE SPIRIT ON THE DAY OF PENTECOST	. . .	79
9	CORINTHIAN GLOSSOLALIA	. . . . .	98
10	MONTANISM: A REVIVAL OF PROPHECY	. . .	113
11	CONCLUSION: THE INVASION OF THE SPIRIT	. .	129

BIBLIOGRAPHY	. . . .	141
INDEX OF BIBLICAL QUOTATIONS, ETC.	. . .	144
INDEX OF NAMES	. . . . . .	149
INDEX OF SUBJECTS	. . . . . .	151

Abstract of The Study

THE New Testament gives evidence of the arrival of Power into human life. The character of the power suggests that God is its author. The name given to that power is the Spirit of God. The Spirit is often associated with abnormal and supernormal phenomena in life; that association is the specific study of the following pages.

There are three sections:

Section One: Abnormal and supernormal phenomena in the religious life of the Old Testament and the New Testament.

Section Two: The contemporary explanation of these abnormal and supernormal phenomena.

Section Three: The significance of these abnormal phenomena and their explanation in reference to specific problems in the New Testament and Early Church.

SECTION ONE

This is mainly descriptive. It is indicated that dream fantasies were supernormal phenomena in the religious life of the Old Testament and New Testament. In like manner one can trace the phenomena of prophecy from the Old Testament to the life of the Early Church. Trance and frenzy were physical accompaniments of the prophetic consciousness. The early *nebi'im* and the 'great' prophets were alike in this. Among other abnormal phenomena mentioned is glossolalia—this is more difficult to refer to in the Old Testament experience, but there seems no doubt that 'speaking with tongues' was linked with the other supernormal phenomena.

SECTION TWO

We remind ourselves that we want to know what the 'people on the spot' thought of this extraordinary phenomenon and how they explained it. It is a *contemporary* explanation and not one in terms of modern psychology. In view of this, there is in this section an introductory note on ideas of Hebrew Psychology. The Hebrew believed in the power of invasive spirits, and this made easy the recognition of the power of the Spirit of God. The Spirit is Life, the Spirit is Power, the Spirit is not flesh—the Spirit animates. Bearing in mind this background of Hebrew psychological thought and explanation, we move on to discuss in more detail 'The Experience of the Spirit'. We suggest that the contemporary explanation of all the abnormal and supernormal phenomena is ascribed to the invasive activity of the Spirit. Since there are good spirits and bad spirits, there is a concluding chapter on the relation between the Experience of the Spirit and Demon-possession. The Spirit is considered to be the Master-power over all other attacking forces.

SECTION THREE

In this section there follows a discussion on various New Testament and Early Church problems in relation to the experience of the Spirit. The first concerns the Day of Pentecost. It is suggested that for the disciples Pentecost meant a revival of the old prophetic consciousness with *all* its supernormal associations —frenzy, glossolalia, and the like. We suggest that the report of events has probably been confused and that the disciples did not speak in foreign languages, but that the glossolalia was ecstatic speech. The greatest event of Pentecost was the 'Uprush of Life'.

Next follows a discussion on Corinthian Glossolalia. We think that the 'tongue-speech' at Corinth and at Pentecost were akin. It is suggested that this particular problem of glossolalia arose at Corinth because of the influence of the Petrine Party, which we suggest overemphasized the 'tongue experience'. Furthermore, we feel that glossolalia came to Corinth via Palestine and Judaism and not via Greece and paganism. 'Tongue-speech' is the association of the Spirit with the abnormal and supernormal.

Now comes a survey of Montanism—which again was a revival of the prophetic consciousness. Montanism has all the marks of the Spirit-possessed prophet—glossolalia, ecstasy, trances, etc. It is an attempt of a section of the Church to give proper place to the experience of the Spirit—in their attempt they became fanatics.

In conclusion, after a brief survey of peculiar manifestations in Methodism and in the Erskine movement, we suggest that the invasion of human personality by the Spirit is associated with the abnormal and supernormal phenomena of life. Those phenomena, however, are not psychophysical like ecstasy and glossolalia, etc., but the phenomena of supernormal conduct, so that the gift of the Spirit is associated with the idea of Perfection. The Spirit brings New Life. This might be the relation of the Old Faith and the New Order.

INTRODUCTION

THE SUBJECT AND METHOD OF THE STUDY

THE New Testament gives evidence of the arrival of tremendous power into human life. A small group of men, ordinary, blundering men, go from a room and become 'the nucleus of a movement that was to turn the world upside down'.[1] Those men said that their disillusionment, depression and defeat had gone, because their lives had been invaded by the re-creating energy of God Himself. In the documents which record this experience the name given to that power is the Spirit of God. The disciples believed that, along with His teaching, Jesus had imparted 'a revealing, life-giving Spirit'. His Gospel, therefore, was not bound to a fixed tradition, but capable of being applied to changing situations with freshness, because it was capable of endless growth. It could 'move with the times', and appeal with attractive meaning to every age. This constant freshness of the Gospel is the freshness of vitality which comes with the gift of the Spirit and is an everlasting reminder that nothing of God's offer of power has been withdrawn from men.

The characteristic feature of the Christian Community of the New Testament is that it is the 'Fellowship of the Spirit'. The Spirit creates and maintains the fellowship. Now, the belief in the Spirit has always sprung out of experience, whether it be the primitive spirit-concept or the New Testament idea. It is natural that such belief has been strongest in times of religious revival. At such times of awakening men have become vividly aware that religious truths which they held because of tradition, were the great realities of life. They have felt themselves possessed by a transforming, uplifting and invigorating power, which seemed to come directly out of a higher world. In the power of the Spirit men have achieved things which seemed impossible, and have become increasingly 'a wonder to themselves'.

The 'Spirit-possession' now, as in the first days, sometimes expresses itself in fantastic ways, but it is none the less significant. Strange phenomena in human life always pricked the

---

[1] J. S. Stewart, *A Faith to Proclaim*, p. 127.

heart and mind to attention, and we find the doctrine of the Spirit in the New Testament associated with peculiar activity. This association has its roots in the old Hebrew environment of the Christian faith. Beginning our study by giving a brief descriptive survey of the most noticeable abnormal and supernormal phenomena in the life of the Old and New Testaments we continue with an attempt to give the *contemporary* explanation of such phenomena. We conclude with a discussion of the relationship of the gift of the Spirit to specific problems in the New Testament and early Church.

This study, therefore, is not by any means a formulation of a doctrine of the Spirit, nor is it an explanation of the doctrine. It is an attempt to discover how the idea of the Spirit is associated with abnormal and supernormal phenomena in spiritual experience and what relationships that has with modern life. We assume that the belief in the Spirit concept was the outcome of a real experience.

SECTION ONE

*Abnormal and Supernormal Phenomena
in the Religious Life
of the Old and New Testaments*

CHAPTER ONE

Dream Fantasies

PRIMITIVE man, observes Dr Langton, appears to have been forced by his own experience into a belief that he possessed a spirit separable from his body, and capable of independent existence. It has been widely believed that dreams and visions which came to him during sleep were largely responsible for the origin of man's belief in his own separable spirit and in those of his fellow men. The primitive mind had no idea of a purely illusory experience. The only interpretation that primitive man could put upon his dreams was that his soul, or second self, had for the time being left his body and roamed at large in the world.[1] During the dream-state man passes from one world to another without being aware of it. The soul leaves the tenement of the body, converses with spirits and ghosts, and at the moment of waking, returns to it again. Yet the life seen in dreams is real life.[2]

In view of the peculiar phenomena of dream experience, dreams have at all times and among all people received detailed attention. This attention is evident in the religious life of the Bible. Lehmann writes: 'In the primitive stages of human development, when all insight into the laws of nature and of the human mind was lacking, dream-images were taken to be actual realities.'[3] Whilst in this section we deal only with a descriptive survey of the phenomena of dreams, it will be good to bear in mind the general remarks on primitive dream-phenomena noted above, and to realize that dreams were not explained physiologically or psychologically.

Abraham had lied to Abimelech, King of Gerar, saying that Sarah, his wife, was his sister. It was through the medium of a dream that Abimelech avoided the mistake of marrying Sarah (Genesis 20^3).

By a dream, Jacob was encouraged in his journey toward

---

[1] Edward Langton, *Good and Evil Spirits*, p. 2, who cites Galloway, *The Philosophy of Religion*, p. 93; also Karsten, *The Origins of Religion*, pp. 57ff.
[2] cf. Lévy-Bruhl, *Primitive Mentality*, pp. 98, 101ff.
[3] *Aberglaube und Zauberei*, p. 414.

Haran. Every Sunday-school scholar remembers the story of 'Jacob's Ladder', when the great vision of the Old Testament was seen (Genesis 28^{12}). Jacob was later helped by a dream when he was rearing a flock ready for his departure. During that same period, Laban was warned through a dream about his behaviour toward Jacob (Genesis 31^{24}).

As well known as the 'Jacob's Ladder' story is the story of the dreams of Joseph. Dream after dream suggested to Joseph his supremacy as a leader of his brethren (Genesis 37^{5,9}). After his capture and imprisonment he secured his release from prison because of his skill as an interpreter of the dreams which came to Pharaoh (Genesis 40, 41).

It was through the dreams of the Midianite soldier about the barley bread tumbling into the camp that Gideon was helped in his campaign against the Midianites (Judges 7^{13}).

Spiritual prowess and wisdom were given to Solomon through the inspiration of a dream (1 Kings 3^{5,15}). Nebuchadrezzar, King of Babylon, was another Old Testament character whose life seemed influenced for good or ill by the dreams which came to him (Daniel 2, 4; also Daniel's dreams, 7, 8).

It is interesting to note that these dreams and others recorded in the Bible are, almost without exception, intended for the benefit of the whole race in general, and not for that of single individuals.[4] Though we are not specifically concerned with the interpretation of the dreams, it is to our purpose to remember that the interpretations of dreams in the Bible are not dependent upon astrology or upon any other occult science, but are simple and ingenuous. Often the dreams are interpreted symbolically. Seven fat kine mean seven prosperous (fat) years, etc. (Genesis 41$^{25f.}$). The recurrence of the dream means that its events will most certainly happen within a short time (Genesis 41^{32}). The dreams of Nebuchadrezzar (Daniel 2, 4) are more fantastic and developed, and the interpretation seems to be more allegorical. It is most interesting to note that in all the interpretations the interpreter believes that he is possessed by the same power, or powers, which inspired the dreamer (Genesis 41$^{15f.}$).

Both in the Old Testament and in the New Testament prophets and dreamers are often mentioned together because of the connexion between prophecy and dreams. Saul inquired of the Lord concerning the Philistine attack and 'the Lord

[4] *The Jewish Encyclopædia*, IV.655.

answered him not, neither by dreams ... nor by prophets' (1 Samuel 28⁶,¹³); hence his visit to the witch of Endor. And from the context it would appear that the absence of dream inspiration was one of the greatest calamities that could have befallen the King.[5] It is significant that in the speeches of Deuteronomy again the prophet and dreamer of dreams are placed together (13²⁻⁴). In the tragic indictments of the pastors and prophets in Jeremiah's oracles, the dream and the prophet's utterance are placed together (23²⁵⁻³²; also 27⁹, 29⁸; see also Numbers 12⁶ᶠ·). When the new revival of spiritual religion sweeps the land, Joel declares that there will be a revival of prophetic power and also a revival of the dream inspiration. 'I will pour out my spirit upon all flesh; and your sons and your daughters shall prophesy, your old men shall dream dreams, your young men shall see visions'(Joel 2²⁸). We shall see later that Peter makes use of this observation to explain the revival of religion which came during the first Pentecost in the Christian era.

In the Old Testament there is not much to indicate the difference between the 'dream' and the 'vision'. It seems, however, that the higher kind of prophet beheld the picture of the dream or vision while awake, either by day or night. Into this category one might place the visions which came to Zechariah where many material and tangible objects became the symbolic representation of actual events (1⁸,¹⁸, 2¹ᶠ·, 3¹ᶠ·, 4¹ᶠᶠ·, 6¹ᶠ·). When Abram received the knowledge that he was going to have an heir, the suggestion is that this vision came during the day whilst he was awake—the horror of darkness being later (Genesis 15¹ᶠ·,¹²ᶠ·). The call which came to Samuel was a call that came at night though the child was not asleep (1 Samuel 3³ᶠ·). It was during the night whilst he was awake that Nathan received the command to take a divine message to King David (2 Samuel 7⁴ᶠᶠ·).

It is clear from these passages already cited that the dream and vision are coupled as the ordinary sources of prophetic oracles. With the great prophets this same idea persists. There is not the same emphasis on the ecstasy in the strict sense of its accompaniments, but there are frequent allusions to times of extraordinary elevation of thought and feeling which become times of illumination. At such times an issue becomes

---

[5] cf. the situation when there was no open vision in the land and when the slightest indication of inspiration was precious (1 Samuel 3¹).

clear, a truth breaks on the mind, a resolution is formed (Isaiah 6; Jeremiah 1⁵). The prophet, therefore, makes the report that he 'sees', 'hears', 'questions', 'replies'—but he makes it quite clear that the pictorial image was not the thing of his own creation or the source of his knowledge. It was the truth which created a vision. Even a verbal message is spoken of as a vision (Isaiah 2^1, 21^2, 22^1; Micah 1^1; Habakkuk 2^2). It may be, however, that such 'visions' are merely illustrations in the preacher's discourse. He does 'see' something which is inspired and is an illumination to that particular point of the discourse under consideration. Some scholars have suggested that the visions of the Old Testament prophets are not genuine, that they are merely prophetical teaching dressed up in picturesque language. It seems, however, that throughout the Bible visions mean 'something seen', and whether at night awake or asleep, or during the day awake, or whether an illustration strikes the prophet—it is definitely interpreted as something seen. That 'something seen' might have a physical or psychical nature. The vision might have become a literary and poetical form consciously employed to embody and communicate truths that have become clear to the inner consciousness—but one can still say that the prophet 'sees' the truth.

The dream or vision phenomena are recorded in one book of the Apocrypha. Eleven chapters of 2 Esdras consist of a series of revelations or visions given to Ezra. Ezra in captivity in Babylon recounts God's favours to Israel in their earlier history, and while admitting their evil heart, yet complains of their subjection to Babylon, which is far more wicked than Israel. In a vision, Ezra receives the answer that he should not inquire into things beyond his understanding (4^{1-20}).

The complaints are renewed. Ezra, by vision, is reminded that the degeneracy of the world is so great that such noble children as of old cannot be produced. The end is coming (5^{21}–6^{34}). Ezra still pursues his inquiry, asking why, if the world was made for us, we do not possess our inheritance. The vision reminds him that the narrow way must be traversed before the large room of the next age be attained. Then follows a picture of the Messianic Age, the appearance of 'my Son' with His attendants and their reign for four hundred years, etc. (6^{35}–9^{25}). After eating herbs of the field in Ardat, Ezra sees a vision of a woman mourning for her son who died on his marriage day. It is revealed to him that the woman is Zion lamenting the fall of her city (9^{26}-10^{60}). The vision is followed by the vision of the eagle (Roman)—the eagle rules until sentence is given by a lion (11^{1}-12^{39}). The sixth vision gives the picture of a man rising from the sea; those who collect to fight against him are burnt up and the man gathers to him 'a peaceable multitude' (13^{1-58}). In the last vision, Ezra sees a picture of his departure from men; to console those whom he leaves he is to write for them two hundred and four books (14^{1-47}). This is in the style of the Apocalyptic which we have seen is used by Ezekiel, Zechariah, Joel, etc., and we shall discover in the main the form which vision-phenomena take in the New Testament.

Turning to the New Testament, the references to dream, vision, or apocalyptic phenomena are not so marked as in the Old Testament. In the story about Jesus which Matthew wrote, he reports that Joseph was informed of the nature of Jesus' birth through a dream (1^{20}). After the birth at Bethlehem it is through the medium of a dream that Joseph is warned of the fury of Herod, and so departs with the family to Egypt. Similarly, when the danger is passed, it is by a dream that Joseph is acquainted with the fact, and moves back again into Israel ($2^{13,19}$).

Perhaps one of the most powerful vision experiences recorded in the New Testament is that of the Transfiguration. It is recorded by all three synoptic writers (Matthew 17^{1-8}; Mark 9^{2-8}; Luke 9^{28-36a}). Matthew reports that when Christ heard Peter, James, and John talking about the experience he called it τὸ ὅραμα (Matthew 17^9), (vision or dream). Matthew and Mark also report that at the Baptism of Jesus the dove, symbol of heavenly blessing and acceptance, was seen, and then came the Divine Voice (known to the Jews as the *Bath-Qōl*).

Luke's story about Jesus starts with a dream or a vision. The announcement that Zacharias and his wife are to have a son in their old age is the message which the vision carried, and the shock of such news takes the power of speech from the old man—thus dumbness becomes 'a sign' of the truth of the vision. Six months later a similar vision came to Mary, and the announcement of the birth of Jesus was made to her—news which she hastened to share with Zacharias and Elisabeth, her kinsfolk. At the birth of Jesus, the shepherds of the fields saw a vision of angels who proclaimed to them the good news that a Saviour was born. Through a vision, Simeon the priest, officiating at the Temple when the child Jesus was consecrated, knew that the baby was predestined to be 'a light for revelation to the Gentiles'; in like manner, Anna, the old widow, knew the special significance of the baby-life being consecrated in that service (Luke 1 and 2).

We may remark in passing that again it is not without significance that in these passages vision and prophecy are closely interrelated. The vision is given and then the words of prophecy are uttered. The prophecy is the result of a vision experience.

One of the early experiences of vision-phenomena recorded in the Acts of the Apostles is the experience of Stephen after his defence speech before the Court of the High Priest. The Court is furious at the so-called blasphemy of Stephen, whilst he declares: 'I see the heaven opened, and the Son of man standing on the right hand of God. . . .' ($7^{54f.}$). The word 'vision' is not used in relation to Philip's departure from the scene of a great revival campaign in Samaria to go to a dreary desert area on the way from Jerusalem to Gaza. However, it seems that the instructions to depart from the scene of triumph and success to start work in a new and unevangelized area came through the medium of a vision experience ($8^{5, 26f.}$).

The vision of Saul on the Damascus Road (Acts 9; also 22^6, 26^{12}; 1 Corinthians 15^8) is one which has changed the course of the world's history. Paul himself suggested that he owed everything to this vision, 'the revelation' near Damascus. It meant for him a completely new beginning, an illumination that shone in the midst of utter darkness: a mighty diversion from, and reversal of, a course which he had previously pursued with undeviating directness (2 Corinthians 4^6; Philippians $3^{7f.}$). There are three accounts of the experience in Acts (9^{3-9}, 22^{6-16}, 26^{12-15}); they vary a little in unessential details, but they all agree in stating that he saw a light from heaven, which he interpreted as an appearance of Jesus, and he heard certain words. The special point in the Damascus Road experience was that he became convinced from that time on that the heavenly Messiah was none other than the crucified Jesus.[6] This vision determined for him his attitude to the crucified Jesus from which the call of the Gentiles into the Christian Church ensued.[7] It was a vision which had a revolutionary effect on the inner life and thought of Paul. Connected with Paul's vision was that which

---

[6] J. Weiss, *The History of Primitive Christianity*, I.191. (English Translation.)
[7] Major, Manson, and Wright, *The Mission and Message of Jesus*, p. 110.

came to Ananias, who was to be the person who introduced the new Paul (late Saul the persecutor) into the community of Christians (Acts 9[10]). Events move rapidly, and in the next chapter Cornelius, centurion of the Italian band, sees a vision which caused him to send for Peter; at the same time Peter, at Joppa, has been prepared for this request, and the mission to the Gentiles begins (Acts 10). Through a vision, Peter receives guidance and escapes from prison (Acts 12[7f.]).

When Paul and Barnabas depart on their first missionary journey, the report of that departure does not use the word 'vision', but it seems quite clear that the plan of campaign was not something merely from the hands of men—guidance came from God, and they were 'sent forth by the Holy Ghost' (Acts 13[4]). They 'saw' the way clearly. For the Old Testament prophet that would certainly have been a vision. That guidance is apparent years later, 'when they were come over against Mysia, they assayed to go into Bithynia; and the Spirit of Jesus suffered them not . . . they came down to Troas, and a vision appeared to Paul in the night; There was a man of Macedonia standing, beseeching him, and saying, "Come over into Macedonia, and help us."' And when he had seen the vision, 'straightway we sought to go forth into Macedonia, concluding that God had called us for to preach the gospel unto them' (Acts 16[7f.]). It was the experience which came through a vision that strengthened Paul when opposition came from the Corinthian Jews (Acts 18[9]). The same courage and guidance came to him through a vision when he was in the storm en route for Rome (Acts 27[22f.]).

When we come to the end of the Acts of the Apostles, we have also come to the end of 'pure' vision experiences. The Book of the Revelation is an apocalyptic book. Its language and character take the form of similar Old Testament and non-canonical writings (viz. Daniel, Zechariah, Ezekiel, 2 Esdras, etc.). The seer sees heaven opened; he sees the sealed book in the hand of God and the Lamb in the midst of the throne. Four seals are opened and four horsemen are introduced; the fifth seal reveals the prayers of martyred saints; with the opening of the sixth seal comes an earthquake which brings destruction and terror. Silence follows the breaking of the seventh seal. Then the seven angels appear, but the sound of trumpets brings more destruction, until the Kingdom of God is established. The seer then sees the effort of Satan to destroy the Messiah at his birth. Out of the sea comes a beast to war against all goodness, but over against evil is seen the Lamb with an army on Mount Zion. Whilst some angels sing the praises of God, seven others bring the last plagues to the earth, the evil city falls and the Messiah appears as the warrior king. The final destruction of Satan is accomplished, and the new heaven and new earth with the glories of its final blessedness are described with joy.

It is not difficult to see links with this work and other canonical and non-canonical books. One hesitates to place such a work among the phenomena of visions, and we shall observe later that when prophecy ceased and Scribism had failed, there was an attempt to make apocalyptic fill the gap. Yet there is no doubt that the seer who wrote the apocalyptic message was possessed of a similar experience to the man to whom the dream or vision came.

Not all men were the recipients of the vision, dream, or apocalyptic experience. It was not something that was usual in the ordinary adventure of life, neither was it an experience that seemed typically human. It was an experience that was unique and all-possessing; it was not normal but abnormal, and super-normal. The real experience was not conjured up, though artificial aids helped; it was an experience that demanded an agency outside human personality. We have seen, too, that the dream or vision came when a divine message had to be given to men, or when special guidance had to be received. The experience of the dream was always associated with the giving or receiving of a special message. We would observe that the vision and prophecy are interrelated, and are often mentioned together; therefore, in our survey of abnormal phenomena, we will next turn to the experience of prophecy.

CHAPTER TWO

Prophecy

INTRODUCTORY

AMONG all peoples who have left any records, there have been persons of extraordinary powers: soothsayers, magicians, wizards, witches, medicine-men, clairvoyants, seers, prophets, and all sorts of persons possessed by abnormal powers. Such people, sometimes called 'divine' and sometimes called 'demoniacs', have played an enormous role in the history of religion—and in human history itself. Dr. Pierre Janet[1] has well expressed the part such men and women have played. 'In the development of every great religion, both in ancient and modern times, there have always been strange persons who raised the admiration of the crowd because their nature seemed to be different from human nature . . . they had extraordinary oblivions or remembrances, they had visions, they saw or heard what others could not see or hear . . . they always carried astonishment, and they played a great part in the development of dogma and creeds.'

When we turn to the specific study of the Christian religion, with its associations in Judaism, we find that from the earliest days there has been a continuous prophetical procession throughout the centuries.

Amongst the Hebrew peoples, prophecy was one of the deepest movements of the human spirit, and its results remained the imperishable heritage of the race. The cardinal fact of the prophetic consciousness is the absolute conviction of possession by an urge that is not explained by mere human energy, and this 'other-than-human' urge produces abnormal psychical characteristics. So much was this evident that sometimes it was suggested that the prophet was a man of unbalanced mind.

Probably the highest conception of the prophet's function is illustrated by Exodus 7[1]: 'And Yahweh said unto Moses, See, I have made thee a god to Pharaoh: and Aaron thy brother shall be thy prophet.' In other words, a prophet becomes the

[1] *Major Symptoms of Hysteria*, p. 8. See Rufus M. Jones, *Studies in Mystical Religion*, p. xxv.

interpreter of his god's commands. This same idea is expressed in Exodus 4[15f.]: 'And thou shalt speak unto him, and put the words in his mouth: and I will be with thy mouth, and with his mouth, and will teach you what ye shall do. And he shall be thy spokesman unto the people: and it shall come to pass, that he shall be to thee a mouth, and thou shalt be to him as God.' The assumption of the great prophets was just that, that no distinction could be made between their words and God's word. There was, however, a historic development in the nature of Hebrew prophecy before it reached those heights. In that development three characteristics of prophecy are always present in some form or other. The one who claims to be a prophet must possess the faculty of 'second sight', 'second hearing', and often there are present the abnormal phenomena of ecstasy. Since there is a development from the early prophet, or *Nabi'* to the later literary prophet, we will consider first the experience of the *Nabi'*.

THE *NEBI'IM*

A typical *nabi'*, or prophet-seer, is Samuel, as portrayed in 1 Samuel 9[1]–10[16]. Saul sets out to look for his father's asses. He and his servant are unsuccessful in their search. When they are near Ramah, the servant says there is 'a man of God' living there, and suggests that they apply to him for information. They find that they have money enough to pay the fee for the consultation, so they visit Samuel. Samuel has previously been in touch with Yahweh, and is therefore able to tell them the whereabouts of the animals which have already been found. Before Saul departs, the seer forecasts several things that will happen to Saul on his return journey. All the prophecies are ultimately fulfilled.

From the story it is clear that second sight and second hearing are under Samuel's control. The Hebrews themselves would not have described it as clairvoyance or clairaudience. From their point of view these things are revealed to the prophet by God himself.[2] He is as mouth and as eyes to his God. People go to him with questions and expect him to get answers at will; there is the implication that the seer is master of his own powers and can work to order. He describes events past, present, or future which are hidden from the ordinary man; he is approached because of his abnormal powers or knowledge on great or trivial matters. It is evident from this story, too, that

[2] cf. 1 Samuel 9[15f.].

Samuel holds a high and honourable position in his town; he has the respect of all about him.

At the beginning of the story there is a most important note (1 Samuel 9⁹). We are told that the man 'now called a *nabi*' was beforetime called a Seer'. That means that the *nabi*' and seer became one.

What was the special characteristic of the *nabi*'? At the close of the narrative in 1 Samuel 10, Saul met a company of *nebi'im* coming down a hill at Gibeah, who were in a state of ecstasy. The ecstasy fell on Saul, also, and so changed was he that his acquaintances were amazed. During the rest of his life he was liable to attacks of the same kind. The word *nabi*' is the word used for these ecstatics. The ecstasy was altogether abnormal. It consisted of behaviour which affected the whole body. The limbs might be stimulated to violent action; there might result wild leaping and contortions. Sometimes the whole movement would be rhythmical, and the phenomenon would seem like a wild dance. At other times the vocal organs were involved; noises and sounds were poured out which were quite unrecognizable as human speech. Bodily features, speech, movements, etc., were so changed that to all outward appearance the ecstatic 'became another man'.[3] An interesting feature of the ecstasy which came upon the prophet is that it was contagious. When Saul met the band 'the spirit of God came upon him, and he prophesied among them' (1 Samuel 10¹⁰). 'Prophesying' here seems to mean the uttering of abnormal words or sounds. On another occasion, the messengers whom Saul sends to take David are infected by prophetic ecstasy when they see a company of prophets headed by Samuel in this ecstatic condition (1 Samuel 19²⁰).

In his ecstatic experiences Saul once, during his wild actions, stripped off all his clothes and lay naked for a full day (1 Samuel 19²⁴). The *nebi'im* collected themselves together in bands and would often act as one man. Those whom Ahab consulted appeared to work together (1 Kings 22⁵⁻²⁸). The 'prophets' of Baal, though four hundred in number, acted practically as one man (1 Kings 18²⁰⁻⁹). The ecstasy of the *nabi*' seems to have been quite spontaneous, though at times artificial aids were used to produce it. Music was used,[4] and

---

[3] cf. 1 Samuel 10⁶.

[4] cf. 2 Kings 3¹⁵. cf. also 1 Samuel 9. The band of prophets had instruments of music, psaltery, timbrel, pipe, and harp.

wines and drugs were most probably used by the Baal prophets. The dances performed in holy places were also a means of bringing on the ecstatic state (1 Samuel 10[5f.]). It is not at all surprising to find that the madman was confused with the ecstatic. The *nabi'* who came before Jehu at the moment of his revolt was called a 'mad fellow' (2 Kings 9[11]).

One of the earliest known non-biblical references to this type of ecstasy comes from an Egyptian story of the eleventh century B.C. It is told in the biography of Wen-Amon, the Egyptian. He was journeying through Palestine and Phœnicia and describes, in detail, a scene of prophetic ecstasy which occurred at Byblos. 'As the king was sacrificing to his gods, one of his noble pages was possessed by the god and fell to the ground in convulsions. . . .' The sequel goes on to show that the ecstatic seizure was prolonged into the night.[5] From that earliest story, in which the traveller Wen-Amon shows surprise at the ecstatic experience manifest by the youth at the court of Zaker-ba'al, king of Gebal, it seems that such ecstasy was a product of Canaan.

The ecstasy was not confined to the Yahweh cult: Edomites, Moabites, Ammonites—all possessed ecstatics (Jeremiah 27[9]). Balaam, the Ammonite, is described as an ecstatic (Numbers 22[4-16]). The prophets of Baal dance round the altar and cut themselves and seem akin to the early Hebrew *nabi'*.

There are women in Israel who show the same abnormal experience of ecstasy—Miriam, Deborah, Huldah, etc. (Exodus 15[20f.]; Numbers 12[2-15]; Judges 4-5; 2 Kings 22[14-20]). The story is told that Moses, in the early days (though the passage was most probably written later), had expressed the wish that there was an urgent desire for more and more *nebi'im*, whilst Eldad and Medad were showing to the community the abnormal phenomena of ecstasy—a state most certainly caught from the seventy others who had 'prophesied' (Numbers 11[25-30]).

We note too that in the ecstatic condition the prophet was able to perform feats which would be impossible to the ordinary man. The Baal prophets gash themselves and seem insensible to pain.[6] After the conflict on Carmel is ended, Elijah runs before Ahab's chariot all the way to Jezreel, presumably because he is still in an ecstatic condition (1 Kings 18[28,46]). It is convenient to remember here that another most interesting feature of the

---

[5] A. Lods, *Israel*, p. 102; also A. Guillaume, *Prophecy and Divination*, p. 298.
[6] cf. the Indian fakir.

activities of the *nebi'im* was their use of symbolism. In some cases the symbolism was merely illustrative metaphor, but usually the symbolic actions were actually performed by the *nabi'* and were regarded as powerful agents for bringing about the event which they symbolized.[7] We shall see that the literary prophets of the Old Testament and the prophets of the New Testament gave evidence of this symbolic action.[8]

Such was the early history of prophecy. These prophets were not individual enthusiasts; they were inspired by common sentiments; they banded themselves together in the early days because they shared a common experience. They animated each other, and as a society reacted on the surrounding population. Their 'prophesying' became like a kind of public worship at the high-place or sanctuary, to which they went up with pipe and song,[9] and those songs had real content.[10] Lods[11] writes: '... there is every reason to suppose that the earliest *nebi'im* may have arisen among the Israelites as the result of contact with and imitation of the Canaanites....' Yet from those beginnings there developed something noble and glorious, an experience which prepared the way in language and experience for the literary prophets who came after them.

THE LITERARY PROPHETS

'In Amos, the oldest literary prophet, we find a religious nomenclature already complete; we find also in him ... the prophetic mannerism and *technique*.... It is not too much to suppose that it was in these "schools of the prophets" that this nomenclature and technique were formed.'[12]

There is a story in 1 Kings 22$^{5-28}$ which tells how one prophet separated himself from the band of prophets. Ahab was contemplating war against Damascus. Jehoshaphat, King of Judah, was with him and they became allies. The prophets were consulted and they, under the leadership of Zedekiah, foretold victory. Jehoshaphat was not satisfied, and asked for more evidence. Micaiah was summoned. At first he gave the same answer as the other prophets, but when asked to repeat

---

[7] cf. 1 Kings 20$^{35-43}$, 22^{11}.
[8] cf. Jeremiah 27^2; Ezekiel; Acts 15^{32}, 21^{10}. W. L. Wardle, *The History and Religion of Israel*, Clarendon Bible, I.174-8.
[9] cf. Isaiah 30^{29}.
[10] cf. 1 Chronicles 25$^{2f.}$; 2 Samuel 23^1.
[11] op. cit., p. 444.
[12] A. B. Davidson, 'Prophecy and Prophets' (*H.D.B.*, IV.109).

his vision he told the truth—that Ahab would be defeated. One man had come out of a band. The band had forgotten its high purpose of pronouncing truth as revealed by experience, and had become a band of 'false' prophets, giving a message which was truth or fiction, so long as it kept them in court favouritism![13] Micaiah stood out, was independent, and this was a certain definite stage in the evolution of the prophet. A century later the individual prophet had become a familiar figure.[14]

The separated prophet, however, was still called *nabi'*. The literary prophet was only different by his independence, and by the tendency to emphasize less the physical manifestations of the prophetic experience. He sought more and more the inner meaning of the experience which came to him. In all else he resembled the earlier *nabi'*. The word '*nabi''* applies to Amos, Hosea, Isaiah, and Jeremiah, just as much as it does to Elijah, Elisha, Nathan, Balaam, etc. The experience of these later prophets was still marked with the abnormal and supernormal. We may take the story of Isaiah's vision. He is in the Temple, but the *nabi'* sees Yahweh Himself attended by winged creatures and fire, he hears voices that are not human. The experience is marked by that of second sight and second hearing (Isaiah 6). Or, again, Amos gives a series of visions which is ecstatic in character. He sees the plumbline and hears voices, or he sees locusts and a basket of fruit (Amos $7^{1-3, 7f.}$). T. H. Robinson[15] makes the suggestion that ecstasy was produced artificially as the prophet gazed at these objects, or as Jeremiah gazed at the almond branch. Robinson goes on to say of the ecstatic experience of Jeremiah, 'There are indications in the actual prophecies which suggest that the experience recorded was ecstatic. . . .

> ' I looked to the earth—and behold, a chaos,
> To the heavens and their light was gone.
> I looked to the hills—and lo, they quivered,
> And all the mountains shook.
> I looked—and behold, no man was there,
> And all the birds of the heaven were flown.
> I looked to the corn-land—and lo, a desert,
> And all its cities were razed away.

---

[13] N.B. Writers of the eighth and six centuries B.C. complain that oracles some prophets gave in the name of Yahweh are determined by national interests (Micah 3^5; Ezekiel 13^{19}).

[14] T. H. Robinson, *Prophecy and the Prophets*, Chap. iv.   [15] op. cit., p. 42.

'The highest poetic imagination could hardly have achieved this. The experience was ecstatic.'[16] In the same way one can safely say that Isaiah, Hosea, Ezekiel, and Zechariah were subject to ecstasy, and possessed the faculty of second sight and second hearing. Perhaps Isaiah has more points of contact with the *nabi'* than the others. He does not disdain the title for himself (Amos does, see below). Isaiah, referring to his wife, uses the term 'prophetess', meaning not that she was possessed of the prophetic gift but that she was the wife of a prophet.[17] He offers a sign to Ahaz. He is known as a wonder worker, able to cause the shadow on the sun-dial to retrace its steps, or to heal the sick prince by means of a fig plaster (Isaiah 38).

When Amos declares with vigour, 'I am no prophet (*nabi'*) neither am I a prophet's son', he means simply what he says. He gives the hint that he was not one of those professional ecstatics, of whom there must have been plenty, who made a living by false prophecy. Here the real distinction seems to be one of character. The ordinary prophet expected payment for his services. At Ahab's court there had been four hundred prophets—an established position. Others were free lances, taking on any customer who required their services. Amaziah, the priest at Bethel, assumes that Amos earns his living in this way by his gift, and tells him to return to Ephraim (Amos 7^{12}). The temptation was to speak pleasant things to their employers and thus retain their favour. The people 'say to the seers, See not; and to the prophets . . . speak unto us smooth things, prophesy deceits' (Isaiah 30^{10}).[18] Amos's utterance, then, does not mean that he dissociated himself from the abnormal experience of the *nabi'*, it means that he will not commercialize his faculties. 'The form of prophecy, i.e. not only outward manifestations . . . but also psychic phenomena, remained essentially the same for new prophets as for their predecessors.'[19]

Before we consider the prophetic experience of the New Testament, we should point out a significant change in the nature of prophecy which affected the outlook of the New Testament towards it. The fall of Jerusalem brought a new spirit into prophecy. We have seen that prophets tended to have an official or subsidized position—whilst others would, in faithfulness to Yahweh, refuse to let patriotic zeal become

---

[16] T. H. Robinson, *Prophecy and the Prophets*, p. 43.
[17] W. L. Wardle, op. cit., I.177.   [18] cf. Jeremiah 23^{16}.
[19] A. Lods, *The Prophets and the Rise of Judaism*, p. 51.

mere chauvinism. In both cases the prophet might pass through genuine psychic experiences. With the fall of Jerusalem and the collapse of Israel as a nation, it might seem that the task of prophecy was ended. For the first class of official prophets this was so—there were no more campaigns to inspire; but there arose those who felt the fate of the nation was bound up with its attitude to a divine law of morality, and these are the men whose words will not perish.

Ezekiel is a representative of this 'second age of prophecy'. His message was accompanied by supernormal experiences and impulses to various symbolic actions. The visions, the weird and often repellent symbolisms, outbursts of terror or rage, were real, and not copied just to fit into a 'prophetic pattern'. His details are sometimes picturesque, sometimes childish; his figures are both elevated and tragic, at other times grotesque and bizarre. Yet, all the time, he is laying the foundations of a new prophecy. He was an ecstatic follower of Isaiah and Jeremiah, but he was much more. There is developed an interest in ritual law and temple procedure, with a prophetic zeal for purity, but he is interested in ceremonial holiness. Some have compared Ezekiel's writing with Leviticus and the *Torah*. There is an alliance between priestly and prophetic ideals. He is preacher and ritualist, theologian and visionary.

For the most part, all that we have of prophecy after Ezekiel until the end of the Persian occupation and after is anonymous and very fragmentary. The voices become less and less. Prophecy in the sense that we have been using it is coming to an end. Writers, seers are passing from prophecy into what is known as apocalyptic. Ezekiel was in this transition period and ritual and law were beginning to take a place beside morality.[20]

Another point to remember as we approach a survey of New Testament prophecy is that during the Greek period of Jewish history (i.e. third to first centuries B.C.), the most characteristic piety was devotion to study of the law. The law becomes supreme in Judaism and devotion to it pervades all forms of Judaism.[21]

THE NEW TESTAMENT PROPHET

We now turn to the New Testament and the question occurs, can one find these characteristics of abnormal phenomena

---

[20] W. F. Lofthouse, *Israel after the Exile*, Clarendon Bible, IV.34-49. Cf. also Harold Knight, *The Hebrew Prophetic Consciousness*, pp. 53-90.

[21] See T. Walker, *Hebrew Religion between the Testaments*, pp. 98ff.

in prophetic experience? To a certain degree the answer is 'yes'.

The New Testament era opens with a revival of the prophetic consciousness. It was a revival because the prophet had lost his earlier authenticity. We have seen that with the fall of the State came the expiration of Prophecy; that at the Restoration 'the law' became supreme for Palestinian Judaism. As we noted, there was the influence of the ritualistic and sacerdotal spirit of the priestly codes. Religious life became a system of institutions, the purpose of which was to ensure the salvation of the nation.[22] In that atmosphere came the decay of prophecy. We have suggested that in the period of Haggai and third Isaiah and Malachi there are further indications of the fall of prophecy, though the book of Malachi closes with a prediction of the return of Elijah. These men became preachers, moralists, who try to instil God's will into minds already familiar with it. They do not proceed from revelation to revelation as did the old prophets; they become advocates of the Written Law, developing arguments, counter-statement and reply, being forerunners of the Scribes and Talmudists. So the age comes when the Scribe takes the place of the prophet; he is the new 'representative man'.[23] Flavius Josephus expresses what was the common idea when he writes: 'The prophets have gone to sleep.'[24] Yet there is a prophetic hope that lives on. 'In future, prophets will rise again and the prophets of the great Lord will do away with the sword.'[25] The Apocalyptic literature is almost silent on this point. In the *Book of Enoch*, however, (Enoch 46³), the Son of Man is portrayed as revealing 'all the treasures of that which is hidden . . .' This promise of fuller revelation seems to imply a personal agent who will revive the prophetic tradition. The prophetic gift is advanced in the *Testaments of the Twelve Patriarchs* (Levi 8¹⁵) as an implicit claim of John Hyrcanus to the Messiahship.

It seems that certain sincere men looked forward to a revival of the glories of the past. They were looking for the advent of a

---

[22] Bousset has made the interesting note that in the time of Jesus the features in popular piety that he attacked are sins to which the legalistic type of religion is specially prone, viz. undue emphasis upon external observances, Sabbath, clean and unclean, etc. On the other hand, of exaggerated estimation of the sacrifices of the cultus, his invective takes little account. His enemies are the teachers of the Law, not the cultus. See *Die Religion des Judentums im Neutest. Zeitalter*, pp. 129f., cited by Box, *The Clarendon Bible*, V.74.

[23] Lods, op. cit., pp. 265–79.   [24] *Contra Apionem*, I.41.
[25] *Sib.*, III.781; 1 Maccabees 4⁴⁶, 14⁴¹.

new Elijah at whose powerful words the divided and rebelling nation would be united and changed. These people nourished their piety on the Old Testament Covenant, the devotion of the psalms, and the hopes of the prophets. The types of this piety are seen in (see below) Zacharias and his wife, 'righteous before God'; Mary, the Jewish Mother; Elisabeth, the woman who believed; Joseph, devout and righteous; Simeon, awaiting the hope of Israel; Anna, serving God day and night. There were many more like them in Galilee and Judea who were continually feeding their aspirations on the prophets and psalms, awaiting 'the prophet' for the salvation of Israel.

Reading the Gospel of Luke, we sense a new spirit of expectancy. Elisabeth, visited by Mary, 'sees' into the future and bursts out into ecstatic song as she declares the truth of Mary's condition. Immediately Mary catches the same spirit and sings the *Magnificat* (Luke 1^{41-55}). At the birth of John the Baptist, Zacharias is possessed with an ecstatic experience, and he also bursts forth into prophetic song (Luke 1^{67-79}). When Mary brings the baby Jesus to the purification ceremony, the old worshipper, Simeon, pours out ecstatic song about the future of the child, and the widow, Anna, is another possessed in this manner (Luke 2^{25-39}). Thirty years move by, then John the Baptist begins his campaign. His ministry is hailed everywhere as a revival of the ministry of prophecy. He was the prophet of the new era. The Evangelists concern themselves with particulars about the Baptist's diet and dress, locusts and wild honey are his food, and camel's-hair shirt and leather girdle his dress. All are indications that John was a member of the prophetic order, for the *Nabi'* was known by such a dress and such a diet.[26] John appeared to be fitting into the old prophetic traditions.

It is important to notice that the coming of Christ was heralded by this outburst of the prophetic gift. We find that few people had difficulty in recognizing Jesus as a prophet. Many suggested that He was 'the Prophet' (John 7^{40}).[27] That was the general view of the ministry of Jesus—'a great prophet has arisen' (Luke 7^{16}). 'This is Jesus, the prophet....' (Matthew 21^{11}; also Mark 6^{15}; Matthew 21^{46}; Luke 24^{19}; John 4^{19}, 6^{14},

---

[26] cf. Zechariah 13^4. Major, Manson, and Wright, *The Mission and Message of Jesus*, p. 20.

[27] cf. 1 Maccabees 4^{46}, 9^{27}, 14^{41}, and Ecclesiasticus 49^{10}; the anticipation of a coming prophet is a marked characteristic of the Maccabean age.

7⁴⁰, 9¹⁷). Moreover, Jesus openly placed Himself in line with the ancient prophets of Israel.²⁸ When we turn to the records of the life of Jesus, the evidence is clear that He had the essential marks of a prophet in the refined and enlightened sense.²⁹

The point to remember is that the Christian era was heralded by an outburst of the prophetic gift. Already there appear the beginnings of an association of the Christian faith with a revival of the prophetic consciousness.

Turning to the correspondence of the primitive Church, we learn that women prophesied in the Corinthian Church, where prophetic powers were to some extent a matter of reputation (1 Corinthians 11⁵). At Rome it was a recognized gift (Romans 12⁶). At Antioch a famine in Claudius's reign had been foretold by Agabus, who came with other prophets from Jerusalem, and among the names of prophets resident there in the normal state of the Christian Church we have those of Symeon Niger, Lucius of Cyrene, and Mnason, besides Barnabas and Saul, who ministered to the Lord in public worship, and received instruction from the Holy Spirit (Acts 11²⁷, 12¹).³⁰ Judas and Silas were two who exercised their prophetic gift at Antioch and elsewhere. At Cæsarea four daughters of Philip, the Evangelist, were prophesying and were later joined by Agabus. Agabus used the old prophetic symbolism, binding Paul's hands and feet and saying: 'Thus saith the Holy Spirit . . . ' (Acts 15³², 21¹⁰).

At certain places in Corinth there is evidence that prophecy was being superseded by glossolalia (see below) and both had run into wild confusion (1 Corinthians 14³³). Paul finds it necessary to urge that not more than two or three should prophesy at the same meeting, and that they should prophesy 'one by one, that all may learn'. Evidently, something akin to the ecstatic condition of the *nebi'im* was being witnessed (1 Corinthians 14²⁹ff.).³¹ In this Corinthian letter he lays down as principles of distinction between prophecy and glossolalia, that 'the spirits of the prophets are subject to the prophets' (14³²), and prophecy was more useful for the edification of the Church and the conviction of unbelievers (14⁵,²⁴). But he distinguishes prophecy also from revelation, knowledge, and

---

²⁸ cf. Matthew 23²⁹ff.; Luke 13³³.
²⁹ For more detailed study, see Note A, p. 24 below.
³⁰ N.B. εἶπεν may imply the ancient form of כה אמר יהוה.
³¹ Weinel, *St. Paul*, p. 255.

teaching (14⁶), and recognizes an order of prophets associated with apostles and teachers (12²⁸ᶠ·). So in the New Testament prophecy ranges from the mechanical utterance of messages up to teaching and preaching, whilst some men were more accessible to the prophetic gift than others. For this reason a class, or band, or order, of prophets appeared early in the history of the Church, of whom were Agabus and others mentioned in the previous paragraph. This was indeed a revival of the 'band of the prophets'. In the Church at Antioch, 'prophets and teachers' seem to have formed one class, and through them was issued the command that Barnabas and Saul should be set apart for the mission to the Gentiles (Acts 13²ᶠᶠ·).[32] We have seen that Peter had the prophetic vision of the universal mission of the Gospel (10²⁸). It may well have been that the prophets were used to supply the impulse and drive to the schemes of the Judaizers when Paul was attacked by this group at Antioch and Jerusalem (Galatians 2¹¹ᶠᶠ·). The prophetic vision came to Paul, for he relates, apparently as one instance out of many 'visions and revelations of the Lord', how he was 'caught up into Paradise and heard unspeakable words' (2 Corinthians 1). Peter read the thought of Ananias and Sapphira (Acts 5¹).

When we move into the period of later tradition, we find it recorded that Irenæus at Rome heard a voice saying, 'Polycarp is martyred,' and at that very hour Polycarp was suffering martyrdom at Smyrna.[33] Ignatius affirmed that the condition of the Church at Philadelphia was revealed to him, and such a revelation had led him to support the authority of the Bishop.[34] The *Shepherd of Hermas* abounds with prophetic visions, messages, and promptings. Irenæus maintained that there were in his time men who had foreknowledge of things to come, and saw visions and uttered prophetic messages.[35] Tertullian advanced, as a proof of his doctrine of the corporality of the soul, the fact that it had been revealed to him by 'a sister whose lot it has been to be favoured with sundry gifts of revelation, which she experiences ... by ecstatic vision, amidst the sacred rites of the Lord's Day in the Church; she converses with angels and sometimes even with the Lord; she both sees and hears mysteries; some men's hearts she understands, and to them who are in need she distributes remedies'.[36] Such phenomena naturally appeared among the Montanists too.

[32] cf. Acts 15³².   [33] Weinel, *Die Wirkungen des Geistes und der Geister*, p. 166.
[34] Ign., *Ad Philad.*, vii.   [35] *Adv. Haer.*, II.xxxii.4.   [36] *De Anima*, ix.

It would seem that this revival of prophecy has been hesitant in expecting a return of the old frenzy of *nebi'im*. There is ecstasy in the New Testament experience, but it is controlled. One would have expected נָבִיא to have been translated by the Greek μαντίς and not προφήτης. Plato in *Tim.* 72.B. distinguishes μαντεῖς from προφῆται, the former being persons who uttered oracles in a state of divine frenzy, the latter being the interpreters of those oracles. This is deriving μαντίς from μαίνομαι, to rage, be furious, to be madly drunk (*Od.*xviii.406), also of Bacchic frenzy (ibid.vi.132)[37]—all of which is illustrative of the experience of the *nebi'im*. Yet in the New Testament this word is avoided, and only once is a cognate word, μαντευομένη, used of the possessed girl at Philippi (Acts 16[16]). As the προφήτης was an interpreter of the μαντίς, there tended to be a blending of the two together, and in the New Testament the προφήτης keeps that meaning of an interpreter of an 'other-than-human' message—something seen and something heard. This is the supernormal and abnormal experience of the New Testament prophet. Later it is suggested that the prophet's proper work is rather edification and consolation, revealing the secrets of the inner life; prophecy is the sign for believers. It is one of the higher gifts, though not abiding like faith, hope, and love (1 Corinthians 13[8]). The prophets ranked next to the apostles, and are even coupled with them. It was not an office to which one was elected, but a special gift that might come to men or women (1 Corinthians 12[28], Ephesians 4[11]).[38]

Then the abnormal experience of the prophet disappears. The period of free, spontaneous, uprushing life has passed. The prophet, speaking revelation in ecstasy, has yielded to the Bishop ruling with authority. Prophecy had degenerated again.[39] There came one great uprising during the first three centuries against the officialism and ecclesiasticism which was slowly taking the place of the ecstatic experience and which was banishing the prophet from the Church. The Montanist movement was that attempt to bring back the supremacy of the prophet.

[37] Liddell and Scott, *Greek and English Lexicon*, also Thayer-Grimm; cf. also Plato, *Ion*, 533-9, in a discussion on poetry, Socrates says that the poet is filled with inspiration by the god. The god's influence is like that of a magnet, it infuses the iron rings which it attracts with a similar power. The poet is not his own master when he composes, he is simply the mouthpiece of the god.
[38] cf. Acts 21[9].
[39] cf. decline of prophecy in Judaism, which we have mentioned *supra*, when prophecy tended to become an artificial cult.

This survey of prophecy will suffice to show that here was something abnormal and supernormal in the life of men. There was some strange 'other-than-human' touch about the man who was a *nabi* or a προφητής, just as there was about the one who dreamed dreams and saw visions. Before we leave this chapter we must make mention of phenomena which sometimes occurred as a man dreamt or saw a vision, or which often came as a prophet was possessed of the ecstatic frenzy, i.e. the phenomena of 'speaking with tongues', or glossolalia.

NOTE A. JESUS 'THE PROPHET'

It is interesting to note that the conclusion that Jesus was 'the Prophet' was founded upon certain evidences and not merely upon tradition. There is no doubt that those who were with Jesus saw phenomena which they related to the prophetic conscience.

There was the transfiguration in which the ministry of Jesus was linked with the old order (Luke 9$^{28\text{ff.}}$). There was the mystical experience of baptism when the voice spoke, and the dove descended (Luke 3$^{21\text{f.}}$); there was the mystical experience during prayer when angels came and ministered unto Him (Luke 22^{43}).

These we have mentioned earlier, but one remarkable point all the gospel writers emphasize is that Jesus had the prophetic gift of clairvoyance. Jesus 'knew what was in man' (John 2^{25}). He knew that the woman in the Pharisee's house was a notorious sinner (Luke 7^{39}). He knew what His disciples had been disputing about on the way, even though they were too ashamed to tell Him (Mark 9^{33}). He could read the character of men.

He was also aware of purely external incidents and events. Before Peter opened his mouth to tell Him so, Jesus knew that the disciples had been asked for the Temple tax, and forestalled his question with one of His own (Matthew 17^{25}). He knew what Thomas had truculently demanded, and showed him by repeating his very words (John 20^{27}). He knew that the illness of Lazarus had proved fatal, and that it was time to go up to Bethany (John 11^{6,11,14}). In the crowd a woman touched His garment. He was touched by many people in a jostling crowd, but He knew that something special had occurred (Mark 5$^{30\text{f.}}$). The Samaritan woman became aware of His Messiahship when Jesus said: 'Thou hast had five husbands, and he whom thou now hast is not thy husband' (John 4^{18}; cf. vv. 25, 29). On occasion He told His disciples what would happen in the future.

There is one point in which Jesus' prophecy differs from that of the prophets, and it is suggested that this is why he is 'the Prophet'. The subject of His prophecy was always and exclusively Jesus Himself (Matthew 21^{37}, $23^{31f.}$, $26^{2,12}$; Mark 8^{31}), men's relationship to Him (Matthew 16^{18}, 26^{21}; Mark 14^{30}; John 6^{70}), and the fulfilment of their destiny in Him (Matthew 8^{11}, $10^{17ff.}$, 24^{2}; Mark 12^{9}; Luke 19^{27}, $^{41ff.}$, $13^{28ff.}$, 24^{49}; John $16^{2ff.}$, 21^{18}, 22). No other prophet ever dared to make himself the subject of his prophecy.

Not only is He Himself the object of His prophecy, but its aim is to be found in Him. By means of it His person is to be established. He told His disciples what would happen before the events took place, and that afterwards they should believe in Him (John 14^{29}). To assure His position as Messiah He produced the proof of prophecy (John 13^{19}).[40] In this respect Jesus is 'the Prophet', for any comparison with the prophets is out of the question. No prophetic utterance ever had as its object the emphasizing of the prophet's own person. He wished to make it clear that Jehovah is God. Unexpected events were not to shake this belief, but to establish it. Jehovah established His own position by foretelling the future through His prophets. Jesus took the place of God. Through His prophecy, faith in Him was to reach assurance.

In the Old Testament in general and in Deutero-Isaiah in particular, prophecy is used as a guarantee of the activity of God. Those who lay claim to divinity are called upon to compete with Jehovah on the basis of 'proof by prophecy' (i.e. using the word prophecy in the sense of foretelling). 'Show the things that are to come hereafter, that we may know that ye are gods' (Isaiah $41^{23f.}$). But the idols cannot do it. 'There is no God else beside me' (Isaiah 45^{21}). Only Jehovah can 'show us former things ... that ye may know and believe me, and understand that I am he' (Isaiah $43^{9f.}$).[41] Is it that the words of Jesus, 'that ye may believe that I am he' (John 13^{19}), are an echo of

---

[40] The connotation of the term prophecy in this connexion means simply the faculty to read character and to predict the future. We do not suggest that in the mind of Jesus there is any thought of the ecstatic phenomena associated with prophecy. It may be that those who associated Jesus and the early Christian Church with the revival of prophetic consciousness looked for ecstatic phenomena after the old pattern.

[41] cf. also 42^{9}, $45^{7f.}$, $46^{9f.}$, 48^{5}.

Isaiah 43[10]? He, like his Father, is giving his people assurance by prophecy: 'I am he.' Peter's denial (John 18[27]), Judas's betrayal, Christ's death (Matthew 26[2]; John 3[14], 8[28], 12[32]), His resurrection, ascension, the coming of the Holy Spirit which was to be in Jerusalem (Luke 24[49]), the fate of the disciples (John 16[2], 21[18, 21]), the acceptance of the Gentiles (Matthew 8[11f.])—all these things demonstrated that He was 'the Prophet'. In Jesus, however, the prophetic experience was of the highest. Ecstasy had its place as he communed with his Father; the prayer reported in John 17 is the moving inspiration of one of those moments. That is the ecstatic phenomenon at its highest. For Jesus the prophetic consciousness was purified. It had little of the abnormal phenomenon associated with the *nebi'im*; it was seeing into men's hearts and interpreting the course of history so as to predict future events. All this is with one purpose—to prove that He is the mighty Lord of history; along with His Father, He is the maker of history (Matthew 26[64]).[42] Indeed, he is 'the Prophet'.[43]

[42] cf. also John 21[22].
[43] See Otto Borchert, *The Original Jesus* (English Translation), pp. 263f.; 428–39; also Charles T. P. Grierson, art. *'Prophet'*, (D.C.G.), II.431–41; also C. K. Barrett, *The Holy Spirit and the Gospel Tradition*, pp. 94–99.

CHAPTER THREE

Glossolalia

'SPEAKING with tongues' is an abnormal phenomenon which is most vividly portrayed in the life of the New Testament community. This has led many to assume that it was peculiar to the New Testament Church, and was a direct result of syncretism with the pagan cults and practices which abounded in the Mediterranean area and particularly in Asia Minor. We do well to remind ourselves that the glossolalia of the New Testament had its roots not in Grecian cults prevailing in Asia Minor but in the ecstatic experiences of the Old Testament prophecies.[1] We saw in the last study how the *nebi'im* were taken out of themselves in ecstasy. The vocal organs were affected; sounds, noises, splutterings, groans, were poured out which were quite unrecognizable as human speech.

In 1 Samuel 10[5f.] we are told how *nebi'im* came down from the high place in an ecstasy. Apart from the wild movements of the bodies of these men, it may be supposed from the context that they shouted in ecstasy, i.e. were 'speaking with tongues'. So the impression arose that a strange 'other-than-human' voice was speaking within them. Something had overpowered them and was crying out of them. It seems that in 2 Kings 9[11], when references are made to the prophet who fired Jehu's revolt, we must think of the prophet speaking with tongues. 'Ye know the man and what his talk was.' Not everybody evidently understood what his ravings and ecstatic utterances were about. The proceedings of such a man needed an interpreter, for not all knew what he wanted.

Sometimes it is suggested that the 'literary prophets' were speaking with tongues. Especially is this so when they are struggling with a powerful stream of words and thoughts which pours out of them at the beginning of a speech. The torrent rushes like a mighty flood. When the unsympathetic hear these outbursts they use the phenomenon as a joke and the prophets become a laughing stock. The adversaries call such language

---

[1] See T. W. Manson, *St. Paul in Ephesus*; Reprint from *Bulletin of John Rylands Library*, XXVI, No. 1 (Oct.-Nov. 1941).

'a dropping of words' (Micah 2⁶; Amos 7¹⁶). Isaiah gives a report which suggests that drunken mockers try to imitate the ecstatic utterances. As the prophet goes into glossolalic speech, so comes the mockery:

צַו לָצָו צַו לָצָו
קַו לָקָו קַו לָקָו
זְעֵיר שָׁם זְעֵיר שָׁם

The prophet replies to such imitated mockery, 'Nay, but by men of strange lips and with another tongue will he speak to this people,' or, as another reading suggests, 'with stammering lips will he speak' (Isaiah 28¹⁰). Here is a very clear reference to glossolalic speech.[2]

In the non-canonical writings, the *Book of Enoch*, the *Apocalypse of Abraham*, the *Ascension of Isaiah* suggest the ecstasy which resulted in other tongues. Enoch is taken into heaven and kneels before God the Almighty. As he kneels, his whole body melts away, his mind is changed, he shouts with a loud and unusual voice, with 'the spirit of power' in this strange tongue he blesses, worships, and magnifies God (*Enoch* 71¹¹; *Ap. Abr.* 17; also *As. Isaiah* 8¹⁷). We discover that each order of angels has his special voice.[3] Volz suggests that this is the root meaning of the phrase ἐν γλώσσαις λαλεῖν.[4] The language of heaven is unintelligible and unspeakable to ordinary men. Only enlightened men may be fit to hear and to reproduce it. The three daughters of Job were provided with a miraculous girdle through which they received 'another heart'.[5] So they become transcendental beings, and are capable of speaking in the language of angels, i.e. of the Cherubim. They sing the hymns of the angels in their own special way.

When we approach the New Testament and view the literature of the Early Church, we have ample evidence that there was an abnormal ecstatic experience which caused certain members of the community to pour out sounds and cries which either sounded like crude 'gibberish' or inarticulate frenzied speech which was 'another tongue'. Sometimes such speech was regarded by those who wrote the report as a 'foreign language', at other times it was just an unknown tongue. At

---

[2] P. Volz, *Der Geist Gottes*, pp. 7ff.
[3] cf. the tongue of angels (*Enoch* 40, esp. *Test. Job*, 48–50). [4] op cit., p. 137.
[5] cf. 1 Samuel 10⁶,⁹. Saul is promised the ecstatic experience and he is given 'another heart'.

the present moment we shall concern ourselves with the descriptive survey of the events recorded and not yield to the temptation which inevitably comes to attempt an answer to the question: 'What was usually meant by the phenomenon "speaking with tongues"?'

The first account which claims our attention is the story of what happened at Pentecost—the story described in the second chapter of the Acts of the Apostles. We cannot isolate the Pentecost experience from immediate events. The Resurrection, whatever it means today, meant for the disciples that every bit of doubt was blasted—all doubt that Jesus was God's Messiah, 'the Prophet', was removed for ever.[6] The Ascension vision was granted to the followers of the conquering Christ—and the conquering Christ was soon to return. Filled with such a hope, a hope tremendously and thoroughly intensified, they returned from the Ascension scene to Jerusalem, gathering enthusiastic eye-witnesses as they went. Some hundred and twenty people came together certain that the exalted Jesus would return at any hour. They bubbled with fervour, eager to share the triumph of Christ. It was in such an atmosphere of vivid expectation, caused by profound religious experience, that the tremendous uprush of creative spiritual power, which we call the experience of Pentecost, came upon them. The enthusiastic and expectant men and women who were gathered in Jerusalem to await what was to come, gave themselves up to prayer, worship, and meditation, recollecting what Jesus had said and done. During one of their gatherings, the people became aware that something extraordinary was taking place. A sound as of a rushing mighty wind seemed to shake the house, cloven tongues as of fire seemed to rest on everyone present, and they all broke out into strange, uncontrollable speech. Apparently prayers, praises, and messages poured out in enthusiastic fervour. Subsequently, we are given the impression that this strange speech refers to foreign dialects and languages, for the report adds that a great crowd of foreigners heard the men speaking and they understood the language. The disciples said they were 'filled with the spirit'.[7]

[6] We do not suggest that 'the Messiah' and 'the Prophet' were synonymous terms. It seems that there is a suggestion in the phrase 'the Prophet' that people were anticipating some sort of revival of the prophetic consciousness that had declined, or that those who wrote the gospel wanted Jesus to be associated with the prophetic experience (see Chapter Two, footnote 40 *supra*).

[7] P. G. S. Hopwood, *The Religious Experience of the Primitive Church*, pp. 141–5.

Something of a similar nature seems to have been the basis of the story which is reported in Acts 4^{31}, though no mention is made of the phenomena of tongues, but the place again is mysteriously shaken after a period of fervent prayer. The story of Cornelius (Acts 10$^{44-6}$), however, is a further report about glossolalia. Peter justified his baptism of Cornelius on the ground that he had shown evidence of the same kind of abnormal phenomena witnessed at Pentecost. For Peter, it seems that the speech phenomena witnessed at the house of Cornelius is the same as that witnessed at Pentecost, and vice versa.

When Paul arrived at Ephesus during his missionary campaign in that district, the community at Ephesus gave evidence that they were in the tradition of the first Christian group, because they too entered into a similar ecstatic experience and also spoke with tongues (Acts 19^6).[8] When Paul writes to the Ephesians he hints that they have ceased to have an experience which once they knew. He exhorts the Ephesians not to be drunk with wine, wherein is riot, but to be filled with the spirit, speaking to one another in psalms and hymns and spiritual songs (Ephesians 5$^{18f.}$). The Epistle to the Ephesians is regarded as a circular letter, and it seems that the people to whom Paul writes such words had knowledge and experience of speaking with tongues.[9] The writer evidently assumed that those who received the letter would understand what he was writing about when he gave such an exhortation. He wants them to find a refined and enlightened ecstatic experience. Again, when he writes to the Colossians (3^{16}) he exhorts them to admonish themselves with 'psalms and hymns and spiritual songs', using the same language as when writing to the Ephesians. At least one can say that Paul is encouraging the Church fellowship to find the glow of an experience that is full of an 'other-than-human' ecstasy and joy. When Paul writes his First Epistle to the Thessalonians he says, 'Quench not the Spirit, despise not prophesyings' (5$^{19-20}$), and it looks as though the apostle in this exhortation refers to the ecstasy that accompanied glossolalia, especially if he linked glossolalia with prophesying (as Acts 19^6). We suggest that for Paul there was no such relationship.

[8] Notice that in this report glossolalia is related to prophecy—'they spake with tongues and prophesied'.

[9] There is no direct reference to speaking with tongues, but the contention is that the tone of the letter suggests that the readers will know something of the experience of ecstasy.

GLOSSOLALIA

In the Corinthian correspondence one of the urgent problems dealt with is the validity of glossolalia in the corporate fellowship of the Church. To know what was Paul's view of glossolalia one cannot do better than read 1 Corinthians 14$^{2-25}$. Here is a translated paraphrase:

'He that speaks in a "tongue", is speaking, not to men, but to God. No man understands, he speaks mysteries. But he that prophesies speaks unto men—encouragement and comfort. He that speaks in a "tongue" edifies himself, the prophet builds up the Church. Now, as far as I wish, you can all speak with "tongues", but it would be better to prophesy. He that prophesies is greater than the one who speaks with "tongues". Suppose I came to you speaking in "tongues", of what profit is that to you? If a flute or harp is not clear in its particular tones, who will know what the tune is that is played? If the "alert" trumpet is not clear, who will be at attention? So, in this case, unless you utter by the tongue intelligible speech, how shall one know what is spoken? It will be like speaking into the air. Every sound has a certain tone, I must be able to interpret those tones—otherwise I shall be like a foreigner. Be eager for spiritual gifts, but seek those which build up the Church. The one speaking in a "tongue" needs to interpret. I pray with the spirit and also with understanding: I sing with the spirit and also with understanding—so over this problem—my wish is to speak five words with my understanding rather than ten thousand words in an unintelligible "tongue", so that I may instruct others also. Please don't be childish—be real adults. "Tongues" are like a sign to those who do not believe; prophesying is a sign to those who do believe. Suppose the whole fellowship were in Church together and everybody was speaking with "tongues", when into the gathering came men uninstructed in Christian ways—men who were unbelievers—would they not declare that you were all mad? But, if you were all prophesying and such people came in, they would hear the intelligible word of God, be convicted and worship God, knowing that God was amongst you....'

From this passage it is clear that to the mind of Paul, glossolalia was speech becoming more and more ecstatic until at last it was entirely unintelligible, so that if any stranger came into the Church whilst the Christian was speaking he was likely to say that the Christian was mad.[10] It would appear that when Paul uses the word 'prophesying' he is not thinking of anything other than a fervent teaching ministry. For Paul there is nothing akin to abnormal ecstasy in prophecy, for it would not be repulsive to the unbeliever who walked into a Christian assembly. On the other hand, we have seen at least one passage where speaking with tongues is linked with prophesying (Acts 19^6). This suggests that there were those who did not have Paul's enlightened view of prophesying. Certain were influenced by old Jewish ideas and looked for tongue ecstasy with prophesying. It is this influence which Paul combats. He suggested that it was better to control the emotional response, retaining the real power of the ecstasy, but expressing it in intelligent prophecy.

We see from this survey that 'glossolalia' was part of the abnormal phenomena in the religious life of the Old Testament and New Testament. It was part of the heritage of Palestinian Christianity. At Cæsarea, Ephesus, Colossæ, Thessalonica, Corinth, etc., this peculiar phenomenon manifested itself. The phenomena were so well known and so well defined as to require no description or comment.

Dream, prophecy, tongue-speech are really all interrelated. We find them all within a similar environment. It is the environment of the tense, mystical atmosphere of silence, or the atmosphere of excitement induced by prolonged musical accompaniment or after an expectant period of worship and prayer. Often the dream was part of the prophetic experience; almost as frequently was glossolalia included in the prophetic reaction. So these three aspects of abnormal phenomena have been considered because they are all interrelated. Not only are they interrelated, but we shall discover that the experience of the dream, the experience of prophecy, and the experience of glossolalia, are all explained as effects of the same cause. An invasion takes place into human personality which immediately results in the abnormal phenomena of dream, prophecy, and tongue-speech, but here we anticipate the ensuing section.

[10] This was often a charge against the Old Testament *nabi'*. The officers of Jehu speak of the prophet sent by Elisha as 'this mad fellow' (2 Kings 9^{11}). Shemaiah speaks of 'every man that is mad, and maketh himself a prophet' (Jeremiah 29^{26}).

SECTION TWO

The Contemporary Explanation of Abnormal and Supernormal Phenomena

CHAPTER FOUR

The Spirit-conscious People

WE HAVE made a survey of certain outstanding abnormal and supernormal phenomena in the religious life of the Old Testament and the New Testament, and we have perceived that there was a certain abiding unity amidst the development. Now we come to the question of interpretation. But care must be taken. If later we would know the significance of these events in religious experience for subsequent history, it is not proper that we should *begin* to explain them by modern psychological technique and procedure. Freud was not a contemporary of Isaiah; Jung did not live in the days of the first apocalyptic visions. Pratt was probably present at revival services in the American backwoods in 1910, but he was not present at the prayer- and praise-meeting on the day of Pentecost. We have our modern experts and their explanations, but it is misleading to *begin* with those explanations. We must start as well as we are able with the explanations sought and given by the people who experienced or saw the phenomena we have described. What did they think about it? How did they explain it all? We are in danger of forgetting that they had not read the most recent work on the Psychology of Religion; we use the method of psychoanalysis, etc., and forget that it was something foreign to the community about which we have been thinking. It may very well be that the psychology of this generation will regard these abnormal phenomena as due to pathological or neurological disturbances. The psychologist and psychiatrist, from the nature of their theory and practice, may explain the abnormal phenomena of religious experience as 'hallucinatory or pseudo-hallucinatory numinous phenomena', and then begin a search for the pathological disturbances. Yet all the time we miss the real importance of the events for the 'people on the spot'. What did they think?

The Hebrew (and this is the environment of the primitive Christian Church) said that God was the explanation of the world. Mr Stanley Casson[1] says of man and his religion:

[1] *The Discovery of Man*, p. 322.

'Religion is man's way of expressing his belief in his approach to God.' The Hebrew conception is just the opposite. It says God has approached man and keeps on approaching him. God comes down to the garden and walks where man walks and asks where man is: 'Where art thou?' (Genesis 3). That is a picture of God which is kept throughout the Bible history. Certainly it is developed and made more glorious, but it is *man* who is chosen. The thought is completed when Jesus says: 'Ye have not chosen me, but I have chosen you' (John 15^{16}).

As Wheeler Robinson[2] says: 'The initiative is with God. We live because He first lived; we love because He first loved.' That was the Hebrew conception of God in history: nothing was done at random, there was a purpose; nothing was left incoherent or chaotic, there was a plan. The initiative remained with God. To achieve this purpose, and to bring into effect His plan, God would break through. He did so, and kept on coming through. (The story of this break-through might be called the significance of Israel's history.)[3]

In the early days, folk interpreted even natural phenomena as manifestations of this break-through. The thunder of a storm meant the approach of God. The law was given on Sinai to the accompaniment of thunders and lightnings, and it was in the calm after a thunderstorm that Elijah heard God; when God came to help this people, 'the earth trembled . . . the clouds dropped water' (Exodus 19^{16}; 1 Kings 19$^{11f.}$; Judges 5^4); or God is approaching in the phenomenon of fire: the burning bush seen by Moses, fire led the Israelites, smoke filling the Temple of Solomon (Genesis 15^{17}; Exodus 3^2; 13$^{21f.}$; 1 Kings 8^{10}; cf. also Ezekiel 1^4).

Earlier thought, too, suggested that God approached through the medium of 'an angel'—not to be confused with the later ideas of 'angels'. G. B. Gray[4] describes this form of theophany as 'an occasional manifestation of Yahweh in human form, possessing no distinct and permanent personality, but speaking and spoken of at times as Yahweh Himself'.

A miracle for the Hebrew is another piece of evidence for this break-through. Even Isaiah is so sure of this that he can offer Ahaz any sign the king may choose in confirmation of the prophet's word (Isaiah 7^{11}), and one recalls that the same Jewish mind asked Jesus to give a sign to establish the fact that God was really approaching the world through Him.

[2] *Redemption and Revelation*, pp. 74f.   [3] ibid., p. 84.   [4] *Ency. Bib.*, Col.5035.

To the Hebrew mind the conception of the triumphant break-through of God into the sphere of human life, this constant coming of God on to the stage of human history, reached its highest thought when it conceived of the event as an operation carried out by the agency of the Spirit. The ideas behind this fundamental belief of the religion of the Bible have a history which is fascinating, but into which we cannot enter. Suffice it to say that the animistic conception of invasive spirits (which flourishes so abundantly in the atmosphere of Babylonian polytheism and demonology) is transferred among the Hebrews into the idea that peculiar and abnormal phenomena in human life and character must all be traced to one source—God, in action by the power of the Spirit. Ultimately, the highest ranges of spiritual experience are conceived to be dependent upon the Spirit's operation. The supreme prayer of a suppliant is that God will not take His Spirit from him (Psalm 51^{11}). Dream, vision, ecstasy, priestly oracle, prophetic word, mighty acts of valour, the glow of prayer and praise, the power of the Christian witness—are all traced back to and explained as an operation of the Spirit.[5]

We may say that the people of Israel and the people of the primitive church—for they came out of the environment of Israel—were a 'Spirit-conscious' people. This Spirit-consciousness in Israel and in the Church of the New Testament has its own psychological history, and before we go on to a discussion on the various activities and manifestations of the Spirit in the life of the people, we shall give a brief outline of the Jewish psychology which was the mental environment of people in the Old Testament and the New Testament.

[5] E. Langton, *Good and Evil Spirits*. (This is a comprehensive study of the Jewish and Christian doctrine, its origin and development.)

CHAPTER FIVE

Spirit in Hebrew Psychology

IN SPECULATIONS about human nature, the Hebrews were realists. What was to them a 'science' we tend to dismiss as poetry or fanciful metaphor. The obvious explanation of the difference between a dead and living man was the absence or presence of breath. In consequence, points out Dr H. Wheeler Robinson, the Hebrews had a theory of the soul which identified the soul with breath. To the Hebrew the soul was not a mystical abstraction: it was the breath. This breath which is the principle of life naturally comes to be regarded as the centre of the consciousness of life and of all its physical or psychical phenomena. The word used for this 'breath-soul' is *nephesh*. It really means life, and that is the best translation of נפש. Elijah prayed for the restoration to life of the child of the widow of Zarephath, and 'the child's *nephesh* returned upon his inward parts and he lived' (1 Kings 17[22]). The idea is 'that the breath animates the physical organs of the body almost like steam setting an engine in motion'. A natural extension of the term *nephesh* is its application to the inner consciousness of life; so we read in Exodus, 'a sojourner thou shalt not oppress, for ye know the *nephesh* of the sojourner, since ye were sojourners in the land of Egypt' (23[9]). 'The usage of *nephesh* could extend to

> All thoughts, all passions, all delights,
> Whatever stirs this mortal frame,

but in practice . . . it was chiefly used of the emotional life and in particular of physical appetite and psychical desire' (1 Samuel 2[16], 20[4]).[1]

There is in the Old Testament another line of approach to the mystery of human personality, viz. that afforded by the term *ruach*, or spirit. This is our immediate concern. It has been said that *ruach* is simply another term for *nephesh*, a synonym for *nephesh*, though with probably a higher range of meaning. To say this is to neglect the important fact that *ruach* is not used of the breath-soul in man or psychical predicates in any pre-

---

[1] H. Wheeler Robinson, *The Religious Ideas of the Old Testament*, p. 80.

exilic passage.² 'The original meaning of the term, a meaning it retains throughout all periods of Hebrew literature, is "wind". From that usage it passed over to denote mysterious wind-like influences, the demonic forces which accounted for the strange and abnormal in human conduct.' Man was always accessible to such influences. The quarrel between Abimelech and the men of Shechem is ascribed to an evil *ruach*. Saul is 'invaded' and becomes a prophet, or later becomes mad; the *ruach* invades Samson and he has supernormal strength (Judges 9²³; Samuel 18¹⁰; Judges 15¹⁴).

In another place³ Dr H. Wheeler Robinson has suggested two main ideas in the psychological beliefs of the Hebrews which we must remember:

(1) they ascribed life and all the phenomena of consciousness to a principle which they identified with the breath (*nephesh*);

(2) they believed in an invasive wind-like spirit (*ruach*) which accounted for anything abnormal in human character and conduct.

The Hebrew idea of human personality is an animated body, not an incarnated soul: and this belief in an invasive spirit made easy the recognition of Yahweh's power. Moreover, the Hebrews ascribed psychical functions to the body—not only to the special organs, such as heart, kidneys, and bowels, but also to the eye, ear, tongue, and hand, etc. So Isaiah and Jeremiah both experience in their inaugural visions a cleansing or consecration of the mouth as the organ of which Yahweh will specially need to take possession.

We can say therefore that in Hebrew psychology:

(A) THE SPIRIT IS LIFE

A live man breathes, so breath is life, so 'the Lord God . . . breathed into his nostrils the breath (*neshamah*) of life' (Genesis 2⁷), and here the word *neshamah* means ordinary normal breathing in contrast to *ruach*, which in this connexion signifies violent, abnormal breathing. Sometimes *neshamah* is paralleled with *ruach*; they are the two aspects of the same divine act, the one the *process* and the other the *result* in life and power.⁴ The

---

² H. Wheeler Robinson, *The Religious Ideas of the Old Testament*, p. 82; also Norman H. Snaith, *The Distinctive Ideas of the Old Testament*, p. 148.

³ *Redemption and Revelation*, pp. 140 ff.

⁴ cf. Job 27⁸, 33⁴ ('The spirit of God hath made me, and the breath of the Almighty giveth me life'—this is a context which we may describe as a key passage. It is clear that 'breath' and 'spirit' have the same significance in the writer's mind.), 34¹⁴f.; Isaiah 42⁵; Psalm 104²⁹f. See Snaith, op. cit., pp. 144f.

well-known passage in Ezekiel shows the significance of this idea completely: 'The hand of the Lord was upon me, and he carried me out in the spirit of the Lord ... he said unto me, Prophesy over these bones, and say unto them ... Behold, I will cause breath (*ruach*) to enter into you, and ye shall live.... Prophesy unto the wind (*ruach*).... Come from the four winds, O breath (*ruach*), and breathe upon these slain, that they may live. ... and the breath (*ruach*) came into them, and they lived.... Prophesy, and say unto them ... "I will put my spirit (*ruach*) in you, and ye shall live"' (37$^{1-14}$). Underlying the prophet's idea of the restoration of a dead or dying people is the conception of the Spirit as the divine organ for the revival or mediation of the principle of life to individuals.

Commencing with the idea of the performance of this function by the Spirit at creation, at the beginning of the race or of human evolution, Hebrew religious thought advanced to the conception of a special intervention of the Spirit as the medium of the animal life of every individual. Through the Spirit, God imparts not merely inspiration for craftmanship or prophecy, for leadership or wisdom, but life itself to every individual. The whole of life can thus come under the domination of the Spirit.

(B) THE SPIRIT IS POWER

The idea of Power is never far away from the word *ruach*. In Ezekiel the two phrases 'the Spirit of the Lord'[5] and 'the hand of the Lord' are for the most part interchangeable. One of the earliest ideas is that a man possessed by or invaded with *ruach* is no longer in control of his faculties. So *ruach* comes to be used of powerful emotions, those dominating emotions that seem to control a man's life. Hosea spoke of a *ruach* of adulteries (4^{12}, 5^{4}). The writer of Numbers 5^{14} speaks of '*ruach* of jealousy'. Human personality could be invaded by these powerful forces. So did the *ruach-adonai* rush upon a man (Judges 15^{14}), or it lifted a man up and carried him away (1 Kings 18^{12}; 2 Kings 2^{16}; and compare the remarkable parallel in the New Testament story of Philip the Evangelist, Acts 8^{39}). The writer of the first chapters of Acts knew exactly what the Old Testament meant by *ruach-adonai*. *Ruach* is strong and overpowering, like the rush and crash of the storm wind. A man can control his

---

[5] cf. Isaiah 11^{11}; 2 Kings 3^{15}; Jeremiah 15^{17}; Micah 3^{8}; Judges 14^{6}, 15^{14}; Isaiah 11^{2}; and especially Zechariah 4^{6}. See Snaith, *The Doctrine of the Holy Spirit*, pp. 24f.

nephesh, but it is the *ruach* which controls him. *Ruach* is associated with storm and tempest and overwhelming might, not warm breezes, or gentle zephyrs. *Ruach* always involves the idea of power—the power that makes the 'cedar of Lebanon skip like a calf', 'that shaketh the wilderness ... and strippeth the forests bare' (Psalm 29).[6]

(C) THE SPIRIT IS NOT FLESH

The Hebrews made the distinction between flesh (*basar*) and spirit (*ruach*) quite firm and clear. The former was from below, the latter from above. An individual was something formed out of dust into flesh; this was invaded and held together by *ruach*, so that for a while it was a breath-soul or *nephesh*.[7] *Ruach* is separate from dust, different from flesh, and in contrast is the source of life and power. The writer of Isaiah 31[3] gave a clear example of this contrast: 'The Egyptians are men and not God, and their horses flesh and not spirit.' *Ruach* belongs to God, flesh is definitely of man, in contrast to God. Flesh has no strength, no power, no life; it is nothing but dust. The other passage which shows the contrast quite clearly and which continually uses *ruach* in almost every shade of its meanings is the passage already cited above, Ezekiel 37[1-14].

So then, in the Old Testament *ruach* is of God and not of man, and *ruach-adonai* stands for the power of God which invades human personality with power.

This, briefly, was the psychological background of the idea of Spirit in the religious life of the Jewish community. We have naturally referred to the Old Testament text, but the same ideas were the inheritance of the New Testament Church. Both in the religious ideas and psychological dispositions which moulded the new faith, the inheritance is Jewish. Throughout the New Testament we see that human personality is still regarded as capable of being invaded. We shall see how the phenomena of demon-possession confronted Jesus at every turn of his ministry. The minions of Beelzebub were indeed dreaded. The demons seized, tore, and choked their victims, made them cry out in agony and roll about and foam at the mouth. The demons clung tenaciously to their human abode,

---

[6] cf. Exodus 15; Job 4[9]; Isaiah 28[6], 40[7]. See Snaith, op. cit., p. 29.
[7] Norman H. Snaith, *The Doctrine of the Holy Spirit* (Headingley Lectures), p. 26; also *Distinctive Ideas*, p. 150f.

otherwise they must wander hither and thither, inhabit unclean beasts, haunt tombs or deserts. The unclean spirit invaded the man and he was under its control. Jesus was the potent one who could bring about the destruction of evil spirits by invading the possessed personality with a stronger 'spirit'—the *ruach-adonai* of the Old Testament.

As we move on to discuss in more detail the experience of the Spirit, we bear in mind this background of Hebrew psychological thought and explanation.

CHAPTER SIX

The Experience of the Spirit

WE HAVE seen that the Spirit of God was first regarded as the Energy which belonged to the Divine Being and we have remarked that the Spirit was considered to be the agent of God's break-through into human life. This Energy, we shall discover, was regarded as being operative in nature and in man. In one of the first creation stories, the Spirit is described as 'brooding' over the formless waste of primeval chaos and evolving from it order and life (Genesis 1^2). The Spirit also sustains and preserves that which it creates, and hence the Psalmist attributes both creation and the renewal of the face of the ground to the sending forth of the Spirit by God (Psalm 104^{30}). We discover that, according to the prophetic picture, the Spirit was to retain these functions in the Messianic age. The Spirit would reconstitute Israel's national life. When the nation was desolate and impoverished it would have to wait 'until the Spirit be poured upon us from on high, and the wilderness become a fruitful field and the fruitful field be counted for a forest . . .' (Isaiah 32^{15}).[1]

We shall now try to discover what was the conception of the Spirit of God in Jewish thought and experience, and then see how that thought was expressed and developed in the faith and experience of New Testament life.

(A) IN THE OLD TESTAMENT

'In the Old Testament, spirit (*ruach*) is fundamentally an activity of God. The word "activity" is used designedly, and in preference to such words as "characteristic" and "attribute". The God of the Old Testament is not "One who IS" so much as "One who DOES", and the essential activeness of God is nowhere more clear than in this idea of the Spirit of the Lord (*ruach-adonai*).'[2] The Spirit is the manifestation in human experience of the life-giving, energy-creating power of God. The writers of the Old Testament and also of the New Testament

---
[1] cf. Ezekiel 37^{14}.
[2] Norman H. Snaith, *The Doctrine of the Holy Spirit* (Headingley Lectures), p. 11.

maintain consistently and persistently that the activity of the Spirit is God's power in and through the lives of men. Because of it, men are able to do those things which of themselves and in their own strength they are incapable of doing. *Ruach* is always associated with life and power, and that life and power belong to God, so that the Spirit or *ruach-adonai* is always a gift to men direct from God. Because of this association the *ruach* of man is also of God, and we have mentioned earlier that no man himself has 'spirit' but only as it descends upon him from God. It comes to man from above, from outside.

(i) *The Experience of the Spirit is the Power of God in the Lives of Men*

The Spirit is the power which enables men to do that which, in ordinary circumstances, is impossible. The Hebrew conception might indeed delete the phrase 'which enables', for they would declare that it was God who was always in action. That thought is very clearly expressed in the story of Othniel's campaign for Israel against the King of Mesopotamia. 'The Spirit of the Lord came upon him, and he judged Israel; . . . and *the Lord* delivered Cushan-rishathaim king of Mesopotamia into his hand: and his hand prevailed. . . .' (Judges 3¹⁰). It was God who did the deed. Or we read, 'the Spirit . . . clothes itself with Gideon' (Judges 6³⁴, R.V. margin). Amasai was possessed in the same fashion (1 Chronicles 12¹⁸). When Samuel anointed David, 'The Spirit came mightily upon David from that time forth' (1 Samuel 16¹³). The Spirit of God was the source of Othniel's ability to judge Israel; in like manner Saul and David were made capable of exercising kingly functions by the power of the same Spirit. The strength of Samson became evident in that moment when the Spirit 'leaped upon him' (Judges 14⁶)³ and he slew the lion with nothing in his hand.⁴

The Spirit of Power was not only evident in a physical strength and kingly ability, it was also witnessed in other unique accomplishments. If one examines the literature of the dream phenomena which we surveyed in the first chapter, one finds that the Spirit is the inspirer of all dreams and visions, likewise the inspirer of all interpretations of dreams and visions.

---

³ The Hebrew צלח is used in the sense of 'rushing'. It is used especially of sudden possession; see also Judges 15¹⁴ and 1 Samuel 10⁶, ¹⁰. cf. Brown, Driver, Briggs, *Hebrew and English Lexicon*. p. 852.

⁴ cf. Judges 14¹⁹, 15¹⁴.

Pharaoh exclaims, 'Can we find such a one as this, a man in whom the Spirit of God is?' (Genesis 41^{38}); he believes that interpretations belong to God (also 40^8 and cf. 41^{16}). Those passages belong to the early Elohist tradition, but in the late Daniel writings one reads: 'There is a God in heaven that revealeth secrets' (2^{28}). Bezalel, the son of Uri, was called in a similar way, and the Lord 'filled him with the Spirit of God, in wisdom, and in understanding, and in knowledge, and in all manner of workmanship', so that he might be skilled to make all the furniture of the Tabernacle (Exodus 31^3, 35^{31}).

It is interesting to note here that Old Testament thought never escapes from the idea of the activity of the Spirit as sudden and spasmodic, and in the New Testament we again encounter it. In one form or another it has maintained itself to this day. In all ages, observes Dr E. F. Scott, it has only been at rare intervals that men were lifted above the customary level of their lives and became capable of great things, and like the Old Testament thinkers they have construed the action of the Spirit by their own experience.[5] Yet though Hebrew thought conceives the Spirit as a power working intermittently, there is a way in which the power is constant. Samson, Gideon, Othniel, Deborah, etc., do mighty deeds on occasion, but there is a sense in which they are always different from their fellows. The prophet Elijah is impelled at intervals to some conspicuous deed, but there is always 'something other' that belongs to him. Or we have the story of the investiture in Numbers 11$^{16\text{f.}}$ where the receiving of the Spirit by Moses and his colleagues is described in detail. The selected men are presented in front of the Tabernacle, Yahweh descends in a cloud and pours out the Spirit, taken from Moses, to the seventy. They show the usual ecstatic signs of Spirit-invasion and possession. Then the ecstasy ceases, the physical accompaniments disappear and do not return, but the men have not lost the Spirit. On the contrary, the permanent possession of the Spirit proved the men to be considered leaders of the people. It is only the ecstatic effects of emotional response which disappear, ecstatic phenomenon that is replaced by a tranquil qualification for their office.[6]

Old Testament thought goes beyond the conception of the Spirit as a mere gust that came and went, though from the

---

[5] E. F. Scott, *The Spirit in the New Testament*, p. 19.
[6] P. Volz, *Der Geist Gottes*, p. 27.

commencement there is always a confusion between what we call the spiritual and the material. So often the physical reactions and emotional disturbances were confused with the real activity of the Spirit as power in the lives of men. That confusion is often encountered in the scriptural doctrine of the spirit. It seems that it was this confusion which Paul tried to combat. The story in Numbers is in experience related to the story in Acts. For the expectant disciples the first moments of the influence of the Spirit are too overpowering. The limitations of the body break, the men are overcome by emotion. That is a physical accompaniment of a spiritual experience. Yet the intended final effect of the experience is not ecstasy, but zeal and ability in leadership; the seventy elders had to become judges, and the disciples ministers and teachers. The ecstasy became rarer, but the Spirit remained with them.

Paul tries to bring out this distinction between the spiritual and the physical in his controversy with Corinth. It is the confusion between the stammering-tongues ecstasy and the experience which produces love, joy, righteousness, goodness, patience, etc. The fruit of the Spirit is love, joy, peace, long-suffering, gentleness, goodness, faith, meekness, temperance (Galatians 5[22f.]). The tongue ecstasy might easily be 'worked up'. The significant thing is that Paul begins with the greatest of the emotions, ἀγάπη, and ends with ἐγκράτεια, self-control—the very thing that is lacking in the physical contortions or noises that passed for the evidence of χάρισμα. This might appear to be a digression, but it is necessary to point out the birth of a conflict in the Old Testament thought which reappears in the experience of the New Testament.

(ii) *The Prophets' Experience of the Spirit*

We have seen that Hebrew thought ascribed every kind of unusual behaviour to domination by the Spirit of God, the power working in and through men which makes men different. The prophet was essentially the person with a difference, and naturally the Spirit was associated with the prophetic experience. In Israel we have noticed that the prophet was originally an ecstatic. We have gathered from the historical books that the prophet was expected to deliver his message in a condition of frenzy and ecstasy, which was sometimes induced or heightened by dances and music, whilst the 'great prophets' speak of their oracles as conveyed to them in a state of ecstasy. What is

THE EXPERIENCE OF THE SPIRIT 47

meant by this frenzy or ecstasy, and how was it explained? They suggest that it is a state induced by the sudden invasion of a force from without. This force, say the prophets, is the Spirit of Yahweh.

Dean Inge writes: 'Ecstasy or vision begins when thought ceases, to our consciousness, to proceed from ourselves. It differs from dreaming because the subject is awake. It differs from hallucination because there is no organic disturbance ...'[7] However, the difference between the Hebrew prophet and the Christian mystic is vast. The mystic is a *seeker* after ecstatic experience. He desires God, and consciously or unconsciously the desire for charismata is present. The prophet, on the other hand, is summoned by God to a definite task and given a definite message.[8] The earliest *nebi'im* believed that in ecstasy God entered into them; this view is undoubtedly influenced by the Hebrew conception of man as a body animated by life, or soul—not as a soul clothed with a body. So in the manner in which Samson, Gideon, Jephthah, Amasai, are 'clothed upon', the prophets are likewise possessed, and the prophetic experience is always associated with the Spirit of God. God's promise (Deuteronomy 18[15ff.]) to raise up prophets in Israel and put His words in their mouth to deliver to the people is fulfilled by putting the Spirit in the mouth of the prophets after Moses (Zechariah 7[12]; Sifre on Deuteronomy 18[18], cf. also *Targum* Isaiah 40[13]; 'Who put the Holy Spirit in the mouth of all the prophets').[9]

The Spirit is the spirit of prophecy, and Guillaume makes the interesting suggestion that philologically the use of the word *nabi'* makes it clear that the experience of the *nabi'* was that of being possessed. 'Philologically the *nabi'* is one who is in the state of announcing a message which has been given to him. He is the passive recipient of something which is manifested in his condition as well as his speech, just as an *"asir"*, a prisoner, is a passive object of imprisonment and manifests his state in his person; or *Mashiah* is the object of anointing and the active witness to this by his life and authority'.[10] For the great prophets, the prophetic frenzy becomes a secondary thing. Probably in the popular mind the Spirit and the prophetic ecstasy were closely connected. The ecstasy could be artificially produced by wild music and frenzied dances, and

---

[7] *Christian Mysticism*, p. 14.　[8] A. Guillaume, *Prophecy and Divination*, p. 290.
[9] G. F. Moore, *Judaism*, I.237.　[10] ibid., pp. 112f.

many charlatans trade upon their supposed possession of the Spirit. Here again rose the conflict seen in the New Testament days, between the physical accompaniments of a religious experience and the real spiritual depth of the true experience. People began to be suspicious of the prophetic ecstasy, often dismissing it as madness (Hosea 9⁷). Just as later Paul had to dissociate 'life in the Spirit' from all forms of mere excitement, so the great prophets were anxious to dissociate their message from all forms of artificiality. Yet, in spite of this, the great prophets do not depart from the conception of inspiration common to the whole of Palestinian thought; for them it is still the invasion of a human personality by a power foreign to it, and they call this power the 'Spirit of Yahweh'.[11] They use terms of closest intimacy, they are grasped by the hand, given the secrets of Yahweh, filled with the Spirit, etc. (Isaiah 8[11]; Amos 3[7f.]; Jeremiah 23[18,22]). The words they speak are not their own but the words of God, through the Spirit, and they accompany them with the formula, כה אמר יהוה—'*Thus saith Yahweh.*'

The full and true prophetic inspiration of the Spirit appears in Micah 3⁸: 'Truly I am full of power by the Spirit of Yahweh, and of judgement, and of might, to declare unto Jacob his transgression, and to Israel his sin.' That is the power of the Spirit in later prophecy. (Moreover, to speak with divine authority brings disaster, cf. Jeremiah 20[18-22].) The Spirit is that gift of power from the Lord by which a prophet is enabled to proclaim the ways of God to men. It is more than an enabling—the prophet is compelled. The testimony of Balaam is a testimony to this urge of the Spirit. 'If Balak would give me his house full of silver and gold, I cannot go beyond the word of the Lord . . . what the Lord speaketh that will I speak . . .' (Numbers 24[13]). Amos experienced that same urge and Micah testified to it also (Amos 3⁸; Micah 2⁷).[12]

In exilic and post-exilic writings the Spirit is still the power by which the prophet is inspired (Nehemiah 9³⁰; 2 Chronicles 15¹ etc.). Jeremiah has few references to the Spirit, but this may be due to the popular tendency to regard the Spirit-possessed prophet as a madman or charlatan. Ezekiel constantly

---

[11] Lods, *The Prophets and the Rise of Judaism*, p. 51.

[12] Jeremiah says his prophetic mission was undertaken against his own desires, 'there is in mine heart . . . a burning fire shut up in my bones . . . I cannot contain' (20⁹). Ezekiel found his calling also a distress but *had* to prophesy. See Snaith, op. cit., p. 18.

speaks of the Spirit as the source of vision and revelation, even suggesting the idea that the Spirit is the agency which transports him from place to place (cf. Ezekiel 11⁵, etc.). For these writers the Spirit will also be the agent in bringing in the New Age of fertility and security; the restoration promised by Ezekiel and by Deutero-Isaiah is to be by the power of the Spirit (Isaiah 11¹ and 61¹ᶠ·), and Christ read the latter selection as a lesson at Nazareth and claimed its fulfilment (Luke 4¹⁸ᶠ·).

For the prophets, the Spirit is simply God acting on men—imparting to them something of His own might and wisdom. For them God is 'the God of righteousness, and the Spirit proceeding from Him is a moral energy, operating for moral ends'. The early *nebi'im* were regarded as inspired and possessed because in their outward behaviour they displayed a frenzy which was plainly abnormal and supernormal, but for the later prophets, though there is always a tendency to ecstasy, the prophet's possession and inspiration is to be measured by his insight into God's will. This is why the New Age will be an age brought to birth by the power of the Spirit. One of the signs of the New Age is that God will pour out His Spirit upon all flesh, sons and daughters shall prophesy, young and old shall see visions and dream dreams, 'in those days will I pour out my spirit' (Joel 2²⁸ᶠ·). The participation in the Spirit-life which had been a reserved experience for chosen leaders will be an experience granted to all the people, and the fervent prayer of the glorious past would be answered: 'Would God that all the Lord's people were prophets, that the Lord would put His Spirit upon them' (Numbers 11²⁹).

In summarizing this section, there seem to be three main lines of Old Testament thought about the Spirit:[13]

(1) *The cosmical, or world relations of the Spirit:*

The Spirit is associated with Creation, with human life as a whole, with intellectual and artistic capacity; with other natural phenomena. The Spirit in the world is concerned with man's physical life, intellectual powers, and executive ability.

(2) *The 'redemptive' relations of the Spirit:*

As in the period of the Exodus, in Judges, and elsewhere, the Spirit is the author of supernormal power and energy coming

---

[13] See W. K. G. Thomas, *The Holy Spirit of God*, pp. 11–14.

on man for the performance of special duties. In the prophets the Spirit is the author of revelation and inspiration. The Spirit is God's gift, often for special work at special times. This unique endowment meant that all abnormal and supernormal phenomena were associated with the action of the Spirit, later the normal prevailed without the accompaniment of excessive physical accessories,[14] though it must not be thought that the later prophets separated themselves from everything ecstatic.

(3) *The individual, personal relations of the Spirit:*

The Psalms and later prophets introduce the ethical and moral aspects of the Spirit's powers. The abnormal is now not so much a physical accessory, but the evidence of a personal supernormal morality. The New Age will be an age in which the common folk will be possessed by the Spirit. The idea of holiness is not directly associated with the Spirit in the Old Testament. It is probable that as the ideal of holiness developed, so the Spirit was conceived as being a Power helping to holiness, for from the later prophets the work of the Spirit can be described as a power to fit men for supernormal service, and the Hebrew would conceive that service to be holy service.

In the Old Testament, then, 'the Spirit' is of God and not of man. For this reason the term 'Holy Spirit' can rightly be used. This Spirit is a condition of life, most of all it stands for power. The Spirit of God is the Power of God in and through the lives of men. The extraordinary experiences in the lives of men are the acts of the Spirit. This we shall see shows itself clearly in the Jewish ideas of Pentecost, and in the story of Acts 2 Pentecost was the day of power, when the operations of the Spirit were seen and noised abroad. This is shown by the early Jewish readings and psalms for the day: Exodus 19; Habakkuk 3; Ezekiel 1; Psalms 29, 68. These five readings all involve a display of the overwhelming power of God, a break-through into human life which is all-powerful and results in supernormal acts. All these phenomena of the coming of the Spirit are also found in Acts 2, except the earthquake, and that appears in Acts 4^{31}. The descent of the Spirit at Pentecost is tempestuous and all-powerful.[15]

---

[14] Lewis Humphries, *The Holy Spirit in Faith and Experience*, pp. 49–51.
[15] Norman H. Snaith, op cit., p. 31; also *Expository Times* (May 1932), p. 379.

THE EXPERIENCE OF THE SPIRIT

(B) IN THE NON-CANONICAL WRITINGS

Dr H. B. Swete says of this period: 'In the non-canonical literature of Palestine, references to the Divine Spirit are rare, and when they occur are little else than echoes—sometimes broken and imperfect echoes—of the canonical teaching. . . . The growing angelology of the Pharisees . . . may possibly have obscured the biblical conception of the Divine Spirit as the operative force in nature and in men. . . . When prophecy ceased, it seemed as if the presence of the Divine Spirit had been suspended or withdrawn.'[16] In the same way, Humphries says: 'So far as the doctrine of the Holy Spirit is concerned, there was practically no advance made. One thing which strikes us, as we read the literature of the period, is the paucity of its references to the Spirit. Moreover, the few which we find seem to be echoes rather than new and living voices.'[17]

In *Tobit* 3^6, the pre-Maccabean book written in Egypt, it is the spirit of a man which ensures his living. The pre-Maccabean and Palestinian book *Ben Sira* follows the Jewish tradition, but we find that the creative function of the Spirit is performed by wisdom (1^9, 24^3). In Judith (Macc.-Palestinian) 14^6, fainting under stress of emotion is described as the failing of Spirit. In 16^{14} there seems to be a parallelism of Word and Spirit (cf. Psalms 104^{30}; Isaiah 30^{18}). The *Second Book of Maccabees* gives the name 'Sovereign of Spirits' to Yahweh, which corresponds to the phrase 'Lord of Spirits' used one hundred and four times in the *Book of Enoch*. There is evidence in this phrase of a developing belief in angels, elemental spirits and spirits of the air, both good and bad. The Palestinian book *Baruch* and the *Apocalypse of Esdras* are all in line with Old Testament tradition, the only developments being those necessitated by the belief in the resurrection and the growing belief in elemental spirits.

It is when we turn to the Alexandrian composition, Wisdom of Solomon, that we find a considerable change. In the Wisdom literature, we reach the meridian of the pneumatology of Hebrew literature before the era of the New Testament. The terms 'Wisdom' and 'Spirit' are equated. The ancient and original description of the Spirit of God was the breath of God: in the context of Wisdom 7^{24-6} is the definition of wisdom as the breath of God: 'For she is a breath of the power of God,

---

[16] 'Holy Spirit', *H.D.B.*, II.404. [17] Lewis Humphries, op. cit., p. 96.

and a clear effluence of the glory of the Almighty.' This equation of Wisdom with Spirit is seen in the following four passages. 'For a *holy spirit* of discipline will flee deceit, and will start away from thoughts that are without understanding. . . . For *wisdom is a spirit* that loveth man . . . because the *spirit of the Lord* hath filled the world, and that which holdeth all things together hath knowledge of every voice' (1^{5-7}); 'For this cause I prayed, and understanding was given me: I called upon God, and there came to me a *spirit of wisdom*' (7^7); 'And who ever gained knowledge of thy counsel, except thou gavest wisdom, and sentest *thy holy spirit* from on high?' (9^{17}); 'For thine incorruptible *spirit* is in all things' (12^1). The importance of these passages is that they form a connecting link on the one hand with the pneumatology of the Old Testament, and on the other with the pneumatology of the New Testament.[18]

There is another lengthy passage in the Book of Wisdom which summarizes the Old Testament story of man from creation to the preservation of the Hebrews amid the wilderness. The Fall, the experiences of Cain, Noah, Abraham, Jacob, Joseph, the flight from Egypt are all described, though not by name, as the work of the Spirit of Wisdom. Wisdom is described as being in charge of the affairs of men (10–12^2). It seems that there is complete identification with the Spirit. As the Spirit endows with gifts, so does wisdom, '[wisdom] rained down skill and knowledge of understanding . . .' (Ecclesiasticus 1^{19}, 15^3, $24^{26f.,32f.}$). With this endowment is coupled the idea of skill in handicrafts as a gift of the spirit of wisdom, which inspires 'all acquaintance with divers crafts' (Wisdom 7^{16}). Moreover, although, as we have mentioned, the age of prophecy seemed ended, the Wisdom writers retained the older Hebrew conception of prophecy as an inspiration by the Spirit of God, and the fact that they attributed it to Wisdom is another indication that the terms spirit and wisdom suggested to them the same idea: 'She foreseeth signs and wonders, and the issues of seasons and times' (8^8); 'She prospered their works in the hand of a holy prophet' (11^1); 'And from generation to generation passing into holy souls she maketh . . .

---

[18] Some have suggested that Luke 21^{15} ('I will give unto you a mouth of wisdom') when read in conjunction with Luke 12^{12} ('for the Holy Spirit shall teach you in that very hour what ye ought to say') is a similar identification of wisdom and the Holy Spirit. It is suggested that there may be a similar identification in Acts 6^{10}: 'the wisdom and the Spirit by which he spake.' cf. A. J. Macdonald, *The Interpreter Spirit and Human Life*, p. 46.

prophets' (7^{27}). In the power to interpret a revealed word, and make clear obscure teaching, there is a hint of the most specific function of the spirit: 'She understandeth subtilties of speeches and interpretations of dark sayings' (8^8). Even spiritual graces and blessings come from the spirit of wisdom and are described in terms that strike the same note as the Pauline list (Galatians 5^{22}) of fruits of the spirit. 'He that loveth her loveth life; and they... shall be filled with gladness. He... shall inherit glory' (Ecclesiasticus 4^{12-14}); 'He shall inherit joy, and a crown of gladness' (15^6); '... the fruits of wisdom's labour are virtues... soberness and understanding, righteousness and courage' (Wisdom 8^7). It seems abundantly clear that in the Wisdom literature, at least, spirit and wisdom are identified.[19] We can see quite clearly, too, that the idea of charismatic gifts is to be traced back to definite Palestinian origins.[20]

So specifically was the Spirit associated with all forms of prophetic inspiration that when the last prophets, Haggai, Zechariah, and Malachi died, some declared that the Spirit had departed from Israel.[21] Then came a gradual move against ecstasy and prophecy. The communication of God, His breakthrough, came through the learning of the scholars and through the Voice from Heaven (*Bath Qōl*), and not through a succession of inspired prophets. The Spirit now speaks not through the prophet but through the scripture, which is the written word. Only a few Rabbis are said to have received the Spirit; Akiba is one of these notable ones.

Josephus may be classed as representing a certain educated opinion and he clearly agreed that the period of Spirit-possession in the experience of prophets had come to an end. Nevertheless, he regarded John Hyrcanus as a prophet, and he explains that John Hyrcanus was visited by the Spirit so that he knew all there was to happen, and describes this as prophecy.[22]

From the non-canonical literature one concludes that beliefs inherited from the past are kept, developed, carried to their logical issue, and often blended with the thought of popular religion. Because there was no great prophetic voice as of old, men tended to feel that the Spirit that made the prophet was withheld. It is remarkable that this thought came into later

[19] A. J. Macdonald, op. cit., pp. 53–64.
[20] cf. Rudolf Otto, *The Kingdom of God and the Son of Man*, p. 343.
[21] *Tos Sotah* 13^2; see G. F. Moore, *Judaism*, I.237.
[22] *Antiq.*, xiii, x, p. 547.

Christianity. When certain signs were lacking, when no one knew ecstasy and the phenomena of glossolalia were absent, when miracles of the abnormal were not seen, the Church insisted firmly that the gift of the Spirit was not given in the same form—just as now men said the prophetic period was closed.[23] Of all the activities attributed by the Old Testament to the Spirit, none had been so impressive as the gift of prophecy. During the period we have been considering the voice of prophecy was dumb, and the Spirit was thought likewise to be inactive.[24]

(C) IN THE NEW TESTAMENT

'The inheritance of the primitive Church is Jewish, both in the religious ideas and psychological dispositions which moulded the new faith. This inheritance carried with it more than religious legalism, theological concepts, and psychological associations; it provided a religious experience of God and the soul which proved to be a noteworthy cradle for the new-born faith.' The religious environment of Jesus, of his disciples, and of the earliest converts to the new community, is all-significant, for personality can never be distinguished from the concrete environing interests and values associated with it. That is why the sketch of the Old Testament experience of the Spirit given above is not something separate and distinct from the New Testament life and thought—it is a pathway leading to it. The religious outlook of the primitive Church was, in many respects, similar to that of Jewish piety and faith, so that it was impossible to be in the realm of one without being within the orbit of the other.[25]

One significant element in the religious environment of New Testament life which we have hinted at in the previous section, is the place and power of the belief in demons. A great change came over Jewish faith after the Exile, in that God was conceived to be more transcendent, using hosts of angels as His mediators; in the same way, God seemed more remote from evil; human suffering and sin were accounted for by demonic agency. The old Hebrew conception that better things could never be without divine intervention encouraged

---

[23] See Foakes Jackson and Kirsopp Lake, *The Beginnings of Christianity*, V, Note IX.

[24] Lewis Humphries, op. cit., p. 98. See A. Marmorstein, *Studies in Jewish Theology*, pp. 122ff.

[25] P. G. S. Hopwood, op. cit., p. 46f.

the belief in evil spirits as responsible for the evils; their power could only be broken by the advent of the Divine Kingdom.

According to Duhm this demonic environment had no roots in the Jewish thought of the Old Testament. He suggests that belief in evil spirits in the Old Testament was slight. Israel was naturally separated from the outer world, and so she was kept fairly free from serious forms of infection from Babylonian and Egyptian Demonology.[26] On the other hand, we read in Genesis (35[4]) that Jacob commanded his household to give up amulets (*nezamim*); they were heathen in character and origin. Centuries later Isaiah declared that Yahweh would remove the amulets worn by women, also the 'nose-jewels'—amulets worn to protect the nostrils against the entry of demons. Then, five centuries later, the man who had been accounted righteous and had died under Judas Maccabæus was found to have worn amulets beneath his clothing—and this was sin (2 Maccabees 12[40f.]). Phylacteries were bound between the eyes for protection, Jewish crests were represented on the door-posts of houses (Exodus 13[9f., 16]; Deuteronomy 6[8], 11[18]). Moreover, the Old Testament recognized demons in *Se'irim*.[27] They were creatures who haunted waste places like the old Arabian Jinn. The *Se'irim* could be worshipped, and possessed their own priest (see Isaiah 34[14]; 2 Chronicles 11[15], Hebrew Text). *Lilith*[28] was a demoness who could cause disease, pestilence, and death. Her work, which was great, was done at night, and she gave her name to a class of demons called *Lîlîn*. Incantation texts about *Lîlîn* have been found inscribed on bowls at Nippur. The bowls were buried upside down at the four corners of the houses, and they held fast any demons which attacked.[29] So it appears that, in spite of Duhm's conclusions, the roots of demonology, which was the environment of the New Testament life, are to be found embedded in all sections of Old Testament thought. The roots had little chance to develop until the destruction of Israel and

---

[26] Duhm, *Die bösen Geister im Alten Testament*. But there is clear evidence of Persian influence on Jewish thought in the use of the name Asmodæus for the chief of the demons. A name borrowed directly from the Persian, Æshma Daeva, the demon of violence and wrath in the later Avesta, see Tobit 3[8], Ἀσμοδαῖος (א) or Ἀσμόδαυς (B). τὸ πονηρὸν δαιμόνιον; Talmud, אשמדיי or אשמדאי, e.g. *Pes.* 110a, אשמדאי מלכא דשידי, Asmodæus king of the demons, cited by T. W. Manson, *The Teaching of Jesus*, p. 154.

[27] See Edward Langton, *Essentials of Demonology*, pp. 39–41, 46.

[28] ibid., pp. 47–8.

[29] A. Montgomery, *Incantation Texts from Nippur*, 9; also W. Robertson Smith, *Religion of the Semites*, pp. 119f.

the Jewish State, and then the number of demons grew incessantly,[30] until in the primitive Church there was room for the belief that demons, evil spirits, were part of an order permitted by God, whilst Christ and Paul speak in terms which seem to suggest the existence of a Kingdom of moral evil in revolt against God. These evil spirits corrupt and destroy the wicked. At their head is *Mastema*, or Satan, or Beelzebub, the prince of demons; the demons and their demon king rule the world as it is, but the divine Kingdom may come at any moment, and that means the end of the demons; the undoing of demonic influence is a sure sign that the Kingdom approaches.[31]

Fear of evil spirits is intense within the background of New Testament life. The plague of demon possession hangs about everywhere. Jesus came with his proclamation that the Kingdom was imminent, and His words were attested by the defeat of demons. When we discussed the principles of Hebrew spirit psychology, we mentioned that they held that human life was readily accessible to the invasive influences of what theologians today might call the supernatural. In Old Testament experience that was how the Spirit came to men. Here again in the demonology of the Early Church we see that idea used and developed. Moreover, the Spirit of God is the power of God in human life which will destroy the demon-spirit. The experience of the Spirit in the New Testament is held responsible for abnormal human character and conduct, and in contrast to all the evil demon-spirits the Spirit of God is indeed the Holy Spirit which operates through human personality. Since such activity seemed always to result in abnormal behaviour, the abnormal phenomena disclosed were still interpreted as denoting the indwelling presence of the Spirit. Normal behaviour did not need any explanation, but just as Joseph's power as a dreamer or interpreter of dreams, or Daniel's skill,

---

[30] Oesterreich, *Possession, Demoniacal and Other*, p. 63.

[31] On old Jewish demonology cf. excursus (No. 21) in Strack and Billerbeck, IV; L. Blau, *Das altjüdische Zauberwesen*, Ch. 1; E. Meyer, *Ursprung und Anfänge des Christentums*, II, Ch. iv.

Billerbeck in the excursus cited above gives a list of designations for demons comprising: (*a*) שֵׁד, the common Rabbinical name; (*b*) מַזִּיק, injurious demons; (*c*) מְחַבֵּל, destroyer; (*d*) פְּגָעִים, spirits of mischief; (*e*) שְׂעִירִים, goat-like, or hairy demons; (*f*) רוּחַ בִּישׁ or רוּחַ רָעָה, evil spirit; (*g*) רוּחַ טוּמְאָה, unclean spirits; (*h*) רוּחַ, spirit. Of these (*a*) represents the New Testament δαιμόνιον, (*f*) is the equivalent of πνεῦμα πονηρόν, (*g*) of πνεῦμα ἀκάθαρτον. Cited by T. W. Manson, *The Teaching of Jesus*, pp. 152f.

or Saul's prowess, or the prophet's power, or the craftsman's skill and Gideon's courage, etc., were explained as being due to the invasive energy of the Spirit, so in the New Testament the power of Jesus, the courage of the Christians, the ecstatic experiences of the early congregations, are due to this same invasion.

As we begin our study of the experience of the Spirit in the New Testament, we bear in mind certain data with regard to the experience:

(*a*) The Spirit-concept is always approached by a way of living experience rather than by any system of teaching. There is no such teaching in Jewish literature.)

(*b*) The Spirit's operation is known through human experience as the divine energy invading and dominating human personality.

(*c*) The presence of the Spirit is evidenced by certain symptoms of abnormal and supernormal phenomena. These extraordinary phenomena lead to the conclusion that they are due to the Spirit's presence.

Such is the environment and background of New Testament thought, and when we turn to the literature itself, the most immediate and striking impression regarding the life of early Christianity is the strong consciousness of the first believers of being under the power and direction of the Spirit of God. When the first Christians looked back to the beginnings of the Church they recalled that Jesus had charged the Apostles not to depart from Jerusalem, 'but to wait for the promise of the Father', which they had heard from the lips of Jesus (Acts 1[4]; cf. Luke 24[49]), and they remembered that he had said, 'Ye shall receive power, when the Holy Spirit is come upon you: and ye shall be my witnesses both in Jerusalem and in all Judæa and Samaria; and unto the uttermost part of the earth' (Acts 1[8]). There are at least seventy references to the Holy Spirit in the Acts of the Apostles; so much is this evident that Wood writes: 'The Spirit manifested itself in every Church and was part of the common experience of many Christians',[32] and another writes of the Acts: 'The book might be termed, "The Acts of the Holy Spirit" in and through Peter and Paul and other leaders.'[33]

[32] *The Spirit of God in Biblical Literature*, p. 157.
[33] Winstanley, *Spirit in the New Testament*, p. 130.

We have referred earlier in the chapter on 'Glossolalia' to the uprush of creative spiritual power which we call the experience of Pentecost. There is no need here to describe the abnormal phenomena of the Pentecostal experience; there was the shaking house, tongues of fire, ecstatic speech. The conclusion reached by the company of disciples is that they were all filled with the 'Holy Spirit', and the abnormal features belong to the thought-forms in which the experience of the Spirit was received. The Spirit was wind-like Energy invading human life. In a later study we shall discuss the phenomena in more detail. This is an opportune moment to state that, in the New Testament, special gifts of speech take the first place among the abnormal phenomena, which mark the gift of the Spirit.[34] As Christ had promised (Matthew 10[20]; Luke 12[12]), the first apostles defended themselves with boldness before the Sanhedrin because they were filled with the Spirit (Acts 4[8]). Stephen refuted the Hellenists, and Paul rebuked the sorcerer, Elymas, through the Spirit (6[10]; 13[9]). The disciples 'were filled with the Holy Spirit, and they spake the word of God with boldness . . .' (4[31]). This has been suggested to be a refined example of the phenomenon of glossolalia, which was the most conspicuous and popular gift of the early years of the Church, but surely this clear, convincing speech is the very opposite of glossolalia. If we refer to all the passages given in the chapter on glossolalia we shall find that the gift of the Spirit was the explanation of glossolalia. Glossolalia seems in the early days to have been the regular accompaniment and evidence of the descent of the Spirit upon believers (Acts 2[4], 10[46], 19[6]), or at least by a certain party it appears to have been the expected accompaniment of being filled with the Spirit. We have observed that it flourished greatly in Corinth, and probably it was common in all or many of the churches of Paul's acquaintance, where it was regarded as a physical and psychical operation of the gift of the Spirit.

Just as all references to glossolalia are explained as possession by the Spirit, so all the accounts of prophecy in the New Testament are explained in the same way. In the Acts of the Apostles, glossolalia, interpretation of glossolalia, and prophecy are all interrelated. Peter recognized in the Pentecostal glossolalia a fulfilment of the promise in Joel, that by the gift of the Spirit all God's people should be prophets. Paul, however,

[34] T. Rees, *The Holy Spirit*, p. 65.

made a distinction. Glossolalia was the ecstatic mood induced by Spirit-possession, finding outlet in unintelligible expression. Prophecy was a direct expression of ecstatic revelation, received and communicated in intelligible form through the power of the Spirit. If we refer to all the passages regarding New Testament prophecy mentioned earlier, we shall discover again that they are all connected with the gift of the Spirit. It is clear, too, that prophecy in the New Testament ranges from the mechanical utterances of messages communicated by the Spirit up to the teaching and preaching wherein the Spirit possessed and inspired the whole mind and spirit of the prophet. From the passages cited in the chapter on 'Prophecy', it would seem that some men were more accessible than others to this gift, and a class or order of prophets appeared early in the history of the Church (Acts 11^{27-30}, 20^{23}, 21^4, $21^{10f.}$). Similarly, the phenomenon of vision in New Testament experience was communicated by the Spirit. The Spirit controlled whilst the real self remained passive (Acts 8^{39}; cf. Ezekiel 3^{14}). Paul's vision, Peter's vision (see 'Dreams', pp. 8ff. above), were complex experiences of the Spirit-controlled mind (Acts $9^{4ff.}$, $10^{1ff.}$; cf. 2 Corinthians $12^{1f.}$). Sometimes the Spirit, instead of communicating its message through the voice of its subject, endowed him with the special power of writing—so John, being in the Spirit, saw and wrote (Revelation 1^{10}; cf. $2^{1,8,12}$, etc.); but the Apocalypse is also called prophecy (22^{18}). The important thing is, however, that its contents are attributed to the Spirit ($2^{7,11,17}$, $3^{6,13,22}$, 14^{13}).

In the primitive Church, then, we see a community of people who believe that their new life of power and service is only explained by the fact that the gift which is the energy of God Himself, His Spirit, has been given to them. The many abnormal accompaniments were only symptoms attesting the Spirit's invasion of their lives. From effects they reasoned back to cause, and realized they were filled with the Spirit who had invaded and possessed their lives. The same energy which would operate in the returning Messiah and bring in the divine Kingdom was in them. There had emerged a company of men and women who were unified by a common experience. The same Spirit animated both the Master and His men.

The abnormal features cannot be put aside as hysteria or pathological disturbances. To the mind steeped in traditional Jewish psychology they were accompaniments of a stirring awakening. Later, the tongues disappear and the ecstatic speech is stopped, they are only the accidentals of a great experience, having no permanent quality. There was always the danger, however, of mistaking the accidentals for the real content of Christian experience. Paul had to warn his Churches against that—that was the problem at Corinth. It was an old danger and problem. We have remarked that it was the Old Testament problem of 'real' and 'false' prophet, and incidentally it is a danger that seems to have been haunting the Christian Church ever since.

It is difficult to find any systematic teaching about the Spirit in the primitive Church, and if we look to see whether Jesus gave any systematic *teaching* on the Spirit to the disciples we are disappointed that there is so little. On the other hand, those who saw and heard Jesus were astonished at His words and works and had no hesitation in ascribing what He did to the activity of the Spirit in Jesus Himself. The extraordinary nature, the unique power of Jesus, led them to declare that the same active energy was in operation, just as the contemporaries of Joseph or Elijah concluded that these were men in whom dwelt the Spirit of the Lord. Everything about Jesus was extraordinary, so it was concluded that in Him the Spirit of God must be at work. The Gospels, therefore, account for Jesus' activity and uniqueness by the Spirit, so Swete writes of the gospel narrative: 'St Luke reveals the fact that the birth of the Baptist was accompanied by a manifestation of the Spirit unparalleled in the life of the Jewish people since the days of the Maccabean. . . .'[35] The birth of Jesus is ascribed to an operation of the Spirit; it is probable that Jesus related His own experience of the Spirit's descent upon Himself at His baptism. It was the Spirit that drove Him into the wilderness; on His return His ministry is carried on in the power of the Spirit. So the Gospels, though not possessing *teaching*, repeatedly give evidence of the Spirit's power and activity (Mark $1^{8ff.}$, 3^{29}, 12^{36}; Matthew 10^{20}, 12^{31}, 28^{19}; Luke $1^{15,35,41,67}$, $2^{25ff.}$, $4^{1f.,14f.,18}$, 10^{21}, 11^{13}, 24^{49}; in this last reference Luke does not mention the Spirit, but unquestionably the Spirit is meant). The bareness of the Synoptic record to the gift of the Spirit does not mean that they were not interested in the gift—it seems that they took it for granted: it was a part of the life of Jesus about which everyone was aware; in other words, the

---

[35] *The Holy Spirit in the New Testament*, p. 12.

'sayings about the Spirit are few in the recorded words of Jesus just because the doctrine was dominant'.[36]

For Matthew, Mark, and Luke, the Spirit was the constant possession of Jesus. It is interesting that Luke alludes most frequently to the Spirit, and when we compare the Gospel with the companion Book of Acts, this prominence to the Spirit is very striking. In the opening of the Gospel everything is ascribed to the operation of the Spirit. It came upon Zacharias, Elisabeth, Simeon. John the Baptist grew 'strong in the Spirit'. In like manner we saw that Acts opens with the great story of the giving of the Spirit.

Some have suggested that the prominence given to the Spirit by Luke is due to the influence of foreign ideas upon him; the facts seem to deny this. Dr E. F. Scott points out that the opening chapters of the Gospel show a clear Palestinian origin and reflect a mode of thinking prevalent in the early community. Moreover, the section of Acts in which we hear most of the Spirit is not that which concerns the Gentile mission but that which recounts the early progress of the community in Palestine. Luke's conception of the gift of the Spirit is the old Hebrew one. The Spirit appears as the power from on high which manifests itself in marvellous action, knowledge of the future, right decision in moments of crisis and perplexity. Luke thinks of the Spirit as presiding over the whole destiny of the new religion, from before the birth of Jesus until the mission had established itself at the heart of the empire, so 'the two books of his history may almost be said to have their central motive in this view of Christianity as the outcome of the work of the Spirit'.[37] One incident in Luke's Gospel is interesting because it might be an indication of what took place in the primitive Church. Luke, as mentioned previously, assumes that the Spirit constantly abides with Jesus, but once he seems to forget this. He tells that when Jesus gave thanks to God, after the return of the seventy from their prosperous mission, He 'rejoiced in the Holy Spirit' (Luke 10^{21}). It is likely that the evangelist is about to record one of the loftiest utterances of Jesus, and 'he recognizes it as similar in character to those ecstatic outbursts with which he was familiar in the Church of his own day. Like the Christian prophets, Jesus was suddenly overmastered by the Spirit and expressed Himself in rhapsody'.[38]

[36] Vincent Taylor, *The Doctrine of the Holy Spirit* (Headingley Lectures), p. 55.
[37] E. F. Scott, *The Spirit in the New Testament*, pp. 63f.   [38] ibid., p. 69.

When we consider the sayings of Jesus reported in the Fourth Gospel, we find they are more numerous than those in the Synoptic Gospels (John $3^{5\text{ff.},34}$, 4^{24}, 7^{39}, 14, 16, 20^{22}). The general idea of Johannine thought about the gift of the Spirit may be summarized:

(1) Christ's departure was to mean the removal of His bodily presence because of the gift of the Spirit.

(2) The Spirit is the special gift of the New Covenant, to perpetuate Christ's spiritual presence among His people and thus continue His redemptive work:
   (*a*) as a revelation of Truth,
   (*b*) as a bestowal of Life,
   (*c*) as an equipment for Service.

There need be no doubt that the Johannine sayings express the mind of Christ, though the author of the Fourth Gospel is writing at a time when Pauline influences had been at work for many years in the Church. We remember that through most of the Churches had gone the conflict of old Palestinian ideas about Spirit possession, linking the experience with all forms of the abnormal and supernormal phenomena. Paul had laboured to bring poise and balance; he endeavoured to settle the conflict by leading to the central truth of the experience of walking in the Spirit. The Galatians are reminded that the fruit of the Spirit is love, joy, peace, longsuffering, kindness, goodness, faithfulness, meekness, self-control (Galatians $5^{22,23\text{f.}}$). The Roman Church is told of the ecstasy of life in the Spirit (Romans 8^9), and is brought into the family of God by the power of the Spirit; prayer is aided by the same Spirit, and joy and peace in believing are brought by that glorious gift (Romans $8^{1-17,26\text{ff.}}$, $15^{13,16}$). The Philippian letter speaks of the triumphant 'fellowship of the Spirit' (2^1), whilst in Ephesians we are told that the believer's zeal, his means of access, his source of strengthening, the goal of unity, is part of the life in the Spirit (1^{13}, 2^{18}, 3^{16}, 4^3). At the end comes the warning: 'And grieve not the Holy Spirit of God' (4^{30}).

With that background the Fourth Gospel has been written. Paul has endeavoured to ease the conflict of the churches, expressed in the Corinthian correspondence, and it seems that the writer of the Fourth Gospel is underlining the main elements of Pauline teaching—continuing the movement away from abnormal accidentals to the real kernel of the experience of the Spirit. Paul consistently takes it for granted that the Church had possessed the Spirit from the beginning. He makes it the test of a Christian man that he must be endowed with the Spirit (Romans 8⁹). When he seeks to convince the Galatians that the Gospel which he first preached to them was in line with the original message, he appeals to the one crucial fact that it brought with it manifestations of the Spirit (Galatians 3²).

We cannot here examine in detail the nature and the scope of all the spiritual gifts which Paul enumerates; but we can note that for Paul the Spirit is operative in *all* the activities to which Christians are called. At first the Spirit's sphere was the abnormal and supernormal acts proper, now there is a wide extension of the sphere assigned to the Spirit; the Christian life in its whole extent was governed by the Spirit. Paul associated the Spirit not merely with particular acts but with the will and temper in which they were done. He believed that by the gift of the Spirit 'men were inwardly transformed, so that their thoughts and deeds were nothing but the fruits of a new nature wrought in them by a divine power. The whole Christian life was in the Spirit'.[39]

It is from this point Paul moves when he develops the thought of the mystical operation of the Spirit upon life, which is everything to his mind. So some suggest that Paul has left the old Hebraic ideas for ideas derived from Hellenistic mystery cults. There seems no fact upon which to found this suggestion; it is merely that with Paul the doctrine which had been in infancy in the early days developed and grew because of the demands of life. Paul understood the moral demands of Jesus. He knew that fellowship with God implies perfect obedience to the will of God; he knew also that will-power, self-control, and human discipline would not lift a man above 'his own shoe-straps'. Some power must come from God Himself and lift men, and the power must be a transforming power. For Paul, the gift of the Spirit is that transforming energy. This is the power from God which effects a radical change, and it is a crucial declaration in Paul's Gospel. For Paul, the gift of the Spirit becomes the energy sent forth from God in order to work in our human nature and transform it into something higher. This is not Hellenistic or new—it is the early idea developed in the Christian faith.

[39] E. F. Scott, *The Spirit in the New Testament*, p. 119.

With all this development it is significant that Paul holds fast to the beliefs of the Early Church. He shows no consciousness that the Spirit in its mystical operation is in any way different from the strange energy that manifests itself in glossolalia and prophecy. He mentions his own possession of these gifts, and declares that the Spirit which bestowed them also has a regenerating power. When we compare this Pauline development with the teaching of the Fourth Gospel we see again how a conception that belonged to an earlier phase of thought was unfolded in its larger possibilities and became the thought that was central and permanent in the Christian revelation.[40]

Everywhere in the New Testament it is assumed that the gift of the Spirit is the power of God in the individual, or in the Church or in the world, and the continued activity of the Spirit was revealed by the presence of marvellous works which were viewed as 'symptoms' of the power operative in the believers. Healings, visions, dreams, tongues, interpretations, prophecies are these symptoms of the Spirit's operations. All these phenomena were the result of spiritual experience which integrated personality.

As the community developed it was realized that hallucination and falseness could enter into such experiences, so Paul and John moved toward the proper place. The community was taught that abnormal physical phenomena were not sufficient, there must be an inner experience which brought forth fruits for life and character and conduct. This became the ultimate test for the experience of the Spirit, not strange speech, etc., but a bold and consistent witness to Jesus unto death and the appropriation of the active energy of the Spirit whose fruits are 'love, joy, peace, longsuffering, kindness, goodness, faith, meekness, self-control'—these are the *abiding* realities within the visions and other abnormal phenomena. The experience of the Spirit is manifested in such qualities of character and ability as wisdom and discernment and the guidance that came to those 'filled with the Spirit'. The prayer atmosphere of the Church was inspired in the same way, and overwhelming joy or courage or comfort was an inner experience that was held within the abnormal manifestations.[41]

---

[40] E. F. Scott, *The Spirit in the New Testament*, p. 131.

[41] There appears in the New Testament a distinction between the Spirit as agent and the Spirit as endowment of gifts, etc. For an enlargement of this idea see Note B, p. 66 *infra*.

The gift of the Spirit then is far more than a pervading influence: it is 'personal, divine power, working directly for ethical and religious ends'.[42] The highest thought is this, that the Christian life derived its power from the Spirit, and it stood so high above the ordinary level of the world as to call for a supernatural cause. The very life of the believer became supernormal and amazing. The gift of the Spirit was the energy of God pulsing within the life of any believer. 'By their fruits ye shall know them.' This was the final test. 'Not everyone that speaks in the Spirit is a prophet, but only if he has the ways of the Lord. By their ways, therefore, the false prophet and the true shall be known.' Thus the *Didache* reflects the guarding principle of the primitive Church. The 'ways' have become the 'symptoms' the possessed one shows.

We may conclude by saying that in the minds of the early Christians the Spirit was conceived as a supernatural power which lifted them to ecstasy, worked miracles, and revealed the secrets of the Most High. These supreme moments commonly came when the Church was assembled together (Acts 4^{31}). The minds of the rank and file, then as now, tended to linger on the unusual, the sensational, the ecstatic, but the more discerning possessed the power to discriminate. Paul saw the supreme work of the Spirit in the grasping of the whole personality by God, and the creation of a new moral life.

There were the naïve popular conceptions about Spirit possession, but from the very beginning there were ethical values included in the work of the Spirit. Boldness of speech is considered to be the work of the Spirit, and other moral virtues are mentioned as being the immediate result of being filled with the Spirit—unity, generosity. Evangelistic power is always connected with the Spirit (Acts $4^{8,13,29-31,32}$, $5^{29,40-2}$, 6^{10}, 7^{55-60}). Thus it would be false to say that even at the beginning of New Testament faith the work of the Spirit is associated exclusively with ecstatic and extraordinary phenomena. There was, therefore, no conscious gap in religious experience between Paul and the early Christian community.[43]

It was this experience known as the gift of the Spirit that was the 'grand depositum' of Paul's faith. For him the Spirit creates us anew and refashions us in Christ's likeness. Life under the control of the Spirit is the life of perfect love; that love is God's

---

[42] Vincent Taylor, op. cit., p. 67.
[43] R. Newton Flew, *The Idea of Perfection*, p. 47

love shed abroad in our hearts. Our sense of sonship is the gift of the Spirit. The hope by which Christians are saved is another gift. The Spirit takes up the task of prayer and prays 'with us'. For Paul, the gift of the Spirit is God's victory in human life. It is the experience which makes it possible for any man to live 'Christ's kind of life', here and now, in Corinth, or Thessalonica, or anywhere. That is a possibility because it is God's will and God's gift.

The primitive Church was a community possessed by the Spirit. In the believers the Spirit worked and produced extraordinary phenomena which in themselves were 'fruits' of the indwelling power. The environment of the early Church provided the vital atmosphere in which the Spirit could operate. In this environment there was a creative religious life and a background of ideas about Spirit-possession. There was no part of life and experience that was not explained as showing in some degree the activity of the indwelling Spirit. Those earliest believers were men of two worlds. Life in the present order was made possible and victorious only because they knew the inspiration of the invading, divine power of a supernatural order. Thus it was that they constituted the new community in which the Spirit moved.

NOTE B. THE SPIRIT AS AGENT AND ENDOWMENT

(a) From Gospels and Acts

Some writers have suggested that the apostles became conscious of the distinct personality of the Spirit only gradually—one ground for this assertion is that when the Spirit was mentioned the definite article in Greek is very inconsistently used.[44] However, a study of the passages in the Greek text[45] where 'the Spirit' or 'Spirit' without the article is mentioned suggests a definite principle of distinction. Wherever the Spirit is referred to as an agent, operating transcendently from without upon Jesus, or upon men—operating, that is to say, as a divine being, the definite article is used. In nearly every case, however, when the Spirit is described as the inward inspiration or impulse or motive of human action, the article is omitted, and the action is attributed to the immanent influence of spirit as energy within the human subject. There are, of course, a few

---

[44] See A. J. Macdonald, *The Holy Spirit*, pp. 65–89.
[45] The test cannot be made by using the English translation.

passages where it is not clear whether the Spirit is referred to as agent or endowment, but these border-line cases do not weaken the argument to be drawn from all the rest.

In the record of the baptism of Jesus, Mark and Luke include the article: '... σχιζομένους τοὺς οὐρανοὺς καὶ τὸ Πνεῦμα...' (Mark 1[10]); '... καὶ καταβῆναι τὸ Πνεῦμα τὸ Ἅγιον σωματικῷ εἴδει ὡς περιστερὰν...' (Luke 3[22]). Here τὸ Πνεῦμα appears to suggest a separate agency. Similarly, the separate agency of the Spirit is declared in Mark 1[12f.]: 'καὶ εὐθὺς τὸ Πνεῦμα αὐτὸν ἐκβάλλει...' Luke's record of this incident gives both usages: 'Ἰησοῦς δὲ πλήρης Πνεύματος (no article); 'καὶ... ἤγετο ἐν τῷ Πνεύματι' (article) (4[1f.]). Jesus was already endowed with 'Spirit'. Compare with this His own claim as he opened the mission at Nazareth. 'Πνεῦμα κυρίου' (no article) ἐπ'ἐμέ...' (Luke 4[18]). It would appear that the Spirit's action as an external guiding or leading agency, quite distinct from Jesus Himself, is noted by the use of the article; but the *condition* of Jesus Himself, i.e. being Spirit-inspired, with a specially endowed human consciousness, is noted by the omission of the article. So also (see Matthew 1[18,20]) in reference to the birth of Jesus, where Mary is endowed with Spirit (cf. also Matthew 12[28], referring to the casting-out of demons by the endowment of Spirit). The disciples are promised the Spirit in moments of crisis (Mark 13[11]; Luke 12[11f.]). The Fourth Gospel maintains the contrast between the Spirit's endowment and the Spirit as an agent in precisely the same way (1[32f.], 3[5,6,8]; especially 7[38f.]): '... τοῦτο δὲ ... περὶ τοῦ Πνεύματος (article) οὗ ἔμελλον λαμβάνειν οἱ πιστεύσαντες εἰς αὐτόν· οὔπω γὰρ ἦν Πνεῦμα' (no article), the contrast again between Spirit as agent and the spiritual endowment which issues from the gift of the Spirit.

It has been suggested that the same uncertainty of the nature and character of the Spirit in the minds of the disciples led them to certain confusion and vagueness in statements concerning the Spirit in the Acts. We have seen, however, that the environment of these writers was one where the idea of 'Spirit-invasion' was part of their psychology, therefore they are not likely to be confused. We find that the writer of Acts uses the same principle mentioned above. (See Acts 1[16], 28[25], in reference to Old Testament inspiration. Again, Peter's speeches, 2[33,38], 5[32], 6[10], 9[31]. Other references are: Acts 10[19,38,45,47], 11[12,15f.], 13[2,4], 15[8,28], 16[6f.], 20[23,28], 21[4,11].) In those passages in which the article is omitted the context shows that the emphasis is laid upon human action inspired by the divine gift, in contrast to the divine agent who inspires with the gift. (See Acts 1⁵, 2⁴, 4⁸,³¹, 6³,⁵, 7⁵⁵, 9¹⁷, 11¹⁷, 13⁹.)

(b) Epistles and other writings

This same general distinction is found in the Epistles of Paul and with the exception of one or two passages it appears that the distinction is clearly maintained.

The endowment of the human spirit with 'Holy Spirit' is to be manifested in new conduct and new endurance (2 Corinthians 6⁴ff·). When Paul contrasts the spiritually-minded individual with him whose mind is occupied with the flesh, the Spirit-endowed condition of the sanctified person is described *without* the article (cf. Galatians 5¹⁶⁻²⁵—in this passage the contrast is between flesh and spirit, i.e. flesh and *human* spirit. The passage does not refer to 'Holy Spirit' at all, and in every case the substantive 'spirit' may be displaced by the adjective 'spiritual' or the adverb 'spiritually').

The several activities of the Christian life are marked by the same distinction. The endowment of the human spirit is described without the article in order to bring out the contrast between the subjective human possession and the objective agent (God) from which it is derived, so '... ὅτι ἡ ἀγάπη τοῦ Θεοῦ ... διὰ πνεύματος ... (no article) Ἁγίου ...' (Romans 5⁵). Paul consistently refers to his own endowment with the Spirit as a gift rather than a personal indwelling, and so omits the article (1 Corinthians 2⁴). Another interesting passage is 1 Corinthians 2¹⁰⁻¹⁴; here the Spirit is described as the agent of interpretation. The article is only omitted in verse 13—but since the whole context is concerned with the personal agency of the Spirit, and since the article is included elsewhere in the passage, it can probably be assumed here, unless the phrase διδακτοῖς Πνεύματος means 'spiritual teaching', or teaching as imparted by and therefore distinct from the Spirit. It would be in perfect contrast with διδακτοῖς ἀνθρωπίνης, 'teaching of human wisdom', and would not require the article. (Other references are 1 Thessalonians 4⁸; 1 Corinthians 6¹⁹; Romans 8¹⁵⁻¹⁶; Ephesians 4²⁹⁻³¹, the gifts of the Spirit; Philippians 1¹⁹; 1 Corinthians 12⁴⁻¹¹, and here the article is consistently used to indicate the agency of the Spirit.) We observe then that from the earliest of Paul's epistles to the latest the agency of the Spirit is denoted by the article.

THE EXPERIENCE OF THE SPIRIT

In the remaining books of the New Testament the same distinction is found; the presence of the article indicates the Spirit's personal agency, whilst human endowment with a gift of the Spirit is described without the article (see Hebrews 2^4, 6^4; 2 Peter 1^{21}; 1 John 3^{24}; cf. 4^5, 4^{13}, $5^{7f.}$; Revelation $2^{7,11,17,29}$, $3^{6,13,22}$, 14^{13}, 19^{10}, 22^{17}).[46]

[46] cf. H. B. Swete, *The Holy Spirit in the New Testament,* Note P, pp. 395ff.; also T. F. Middleton, *The Doctrine of the Greek Article applied to the Criticism and Illustration of the New Testament* (cited by R. Birch Hoyle, *The Holy Spirit in St Paul,* p. 181, Note I).

CHAPTER SEVEN

The Experience of Spirit- and Demon-Possession

REFERENCE has been made in the previous chapter to the evidence in the New Testament which points to a belief in the reality and activity of demons.[1] We discovered that certain abnormal and supernormal phenomena were attached to demon activity. However unscientific this concept of demon possession might appear to the modern mind, it is a concept often encountered in the Gospel record. We are not here concerned with an interpretation or further factual review of the phenomena; such a study has been given by Dr Edward Langton.[2] Our immediate concern is an examination of the relationship between what is known as the experience of the Spirit and that of demon-possession.[3]

The similarity of 'symptoms' in spirit- and demon-possession is evidenced by certain criticisms levelled at Jesus by the scribes and Pharisees. Faced with the task of explaining the extraordinary achievements of the ministry of Jesus these opponents suggested that He was possessed by the prince of demons (Luke 11^{14}; cf. Matthew 9^{34}, 10^{25}, 12^{24}; Mark 3^{22}, etc.).[4] Such criticism obviously would have been foolish had there been no similarity of symptoms in spirit- and demon-possession.

It would appear that phenomena which were inspired by the Spirit might be interpreted as due to demons; on the other hand, the opposite might happen, and phenomena really demonic were sometimes misread as coming from the Spirit. Hence there arose the need for what Paul called 'discerning of spirits' (1 Corinthians 12^{10}). Admittedly Paul's reference here was to the faculty of testing whether the ecstatic utterances of a worshipper came from the Holy Spirit or from some inferior source.[5] There is little doubt, however, that the art of discerning

---

[1] *supra*, p. 54.
[2] See *Essentials of Demonology* and *Good and Evil Spirits*.
[3] Dr P. G. S. Hopwood has an interesting study of this question in *The Religious Experience of the Primitive Church*, pp. 197-206.
[4] Similar charges were made against John the Baptist (Matthew 11^{18}).
[5] cf. G. W. Butterworth, *Spiritualism and Religion*, p. 94.

spirits had wider application for 'there is always need of proving that which is spoken under spiritual influence, because a lying spirit, sent by the devil, can also inspire men and deceive the Church'.

Demon-possession took various forms. The victim might be deprived of speech or sight (Matthew $9^{32f.}$, 12^{22}; Luke 11^{14}, etc.). Often the mere fact of possession is mentioned without further details, but always the implication is that a breakdown in mental or physical health is associated with the demon (Matthew 4^{24}, 15^{22-8}; Mark 1 ^{32,34,39} $3^{11f.}$; Luke 4^{41}, 6^{18}, 7^{21}). Sometimes more than one demon could possess a man. One reported incident (Luke 8^{27-39}) reveals the possessed one endowed with abnormal strength.[6]

The Gospels undoubtedly show that human personality can be the scene of activity for the Spirit and demons alike.[7] The organs of speech can be used by the Spirit, or on the other hand an indwelling demon may control the utterances of the possessed. There are 'the groanings which cannot be uttered', enabling a man in his prayer-life to cry 'Abba, Father', which are the inspiration of the Spirit; the demons however may cause their victims to curse and mock. The Spirit on occasion impels men to action, even against their own inclinations or desires; Philip is sent to Gaza (Acts 8^{26}); Paul is hindered and then driven to Macedonia (Acts $16^{7f.}$). Similar, seemingly irresistible urges (but this time toward evil) are the result of demon-possession: the demon 'seizes', 'holds' a person or drives its victim out of human habitation. We have already pointed out that demon-possession resulted in strange marvels in physical strength. Ecstatic conduct, which was often regarded as a sign of the Spirit's presence, was paralleled in demon-possession by the victim being 'beside himself' or 'mad'. Furthermore, just as the Spirit conferred superhuman insight and wisdom, so a strange uncanny discernment resulted from demon-possession (Luke $4^{34,41}$, 8^{31}).

We have already observed that the Hebrews regarded human personality as capable of invasion by a supernatural power. It is precisely such a psychology of religious experience which accounts for the resemblances between the two orders of 'spirit experience'. As a man believed himself to have the Spirit, so at other times he might hold the conviction that he was demon-

---

[6] cf. the endowment of strength given to the Spirit-possessed.
[7] cf. P. G. S. Hopwood, *The Religious Experience of the Primitive Church*, pp. 198f.

possessed. The symptoms of both experiences, as we have observed, often showed certain similarities.

The Gospels show that Christ put Himself in combat against the demons, and made it one of His chief aims to overthrow their Kingdom.[8] According to Matthew 10[1] special powers were given to the apostles to enable them to exorcise demons, and it is noteworthy that Peter when describing the Mission of Christ stresses this very point (Acts 10[38]). That the 'casting out of demons' was significant in the mind of Christ is surely underlined by the fact that He directly appeals to His power over evil spirits as a proof of His Messiahship (Luke 11[20]). There is evidence that Paul made use of the exorcising power at Philippi (Acts 16[16-18])[9] and also at Ephesus (Acts 19[11f.]).

We have therefore in the New Testament a situation in which the existence of demons under the rule of their prince was taken as axiomatic, and all in open rebellion against God.[10]

Faced with this aggressive problem we have noted that the primitive Church in dealing with it used the concept of the counter-acting power of the mighty Spirit of God. The demons, having invaded personality, could be expelled by a stronger power. The Spirit of God was regarded as that conquering master power. Those who were possessed by the Spirit, asserts P. G. S. Hopwood,[11] had within themselves the spiritual power that could bring harmony and healing to the demon-possessed. The demon was expelled by the power of the Holy Spirit and healing took place when the Holy Spirit took possession of the personality once claimed by demons. Human personality could not be possessed at one and the same time by the Spirit and by a demon. The change that had to be accomplished was from the experience denoted by 'he has a demon' or 'he has an unclean spirit' to the state suggested in the phrase 'the Holy Spirit is upon him', i.e. from demon-possession to Spirit-possession.

The similarities between the two experiences we have been considering, of spirit- and demon-possession, are not accidental. Dr Hopwood[12] underlines interesting connecting links. At one

---

[8] cf. Art. 'Demons', W. O. E. Oesterley (*D.C.G.*), I.442.
[9] The word used for a *pythonical* spirit in reference to the girl is found nowhere else in the New Testament. Wherever it is used in the Septuagint it is invariably of sayings of lying prophets or those who practised arts forbidden by Jewish Law (Samuel 28). See Thayer-Grimm, *Lexicon*, p. 557.
[10] Hopwood, op. cit., p. 200.   [11] ibid., p. 201.   [12] ibid., p. 202.

time in the thought of the Hebrews, both experiences were ascribed to the agency of God. God 'sends' an evil spirit which causes the men of Shechem to deal treacherously with Abimilech (Judges 9^{23}); the attempt on David's life is thought to be due to the evil spirit influencing Saul (1 Samuel 18^{10}). 'Lying' spirits cause prophets to utter false predictions (1 Kings 22^{23}). These ideas are repeated by the later Jewish historians in Chronicles, which suggests that at the later period the idea had not been revised since they were retained as explanations. The Levites pray and call to remembrance how God gave His 'good' spirit to instruct the people in the wilderness (Nehemiah 9^{20}). Some may infer that this means that God could give an 'evil' spirit if He wished.

A century or so prior to the coming of Jesus there is a suggestion of a change in interpretation. A whole series of evil spirits is held responsible for the evil works and dispositions of men. According to the *Book of Enoch*, the demons are lost angels. These evil spirits 'afflict, oppress, destroy, attack, do battle and work destruction on the earth and cause trouble' (1 Enoch $15^{9f.}$). They assume 'many different forms' and 'defile mankind' (1 Enoch 19^1). In the *Testaments of the Twelve Patriarchs* we are informed that evil spirits of fornication, gluttony, flattery, pride, falsehood, and injustice, are sent out from Beliar against mankind. The inference seems to be that abnormal delinquencies are accounted for by the invasion of the demons.[13]

Dr Hopwood[14] in his study points out that as the evil spirits are thus being dissociated from the divine source there is a parallel movement which tends to remove the experience of the Holy Spirit from association with demonic effects. Thus, we have reference to the 'spirit of wisdom', the 'faithful spirit', the 'excellent spirit', the 'spirit of judgement', the 'spirit of grace', the 'spirit of discipline', etc. (cf. Wisdom 1^5, 7^7, Ecclesiasticus 39^6, etc.). The process continues, and only qualities related to the good life are associated with the experience of the Spirit: their source is seen as God. Thus we have the 'spirit of faith' (1 Enoch 61^{11}), the 'spirit of peace' (1 Enoch 61^{11}) the 'spirit of goodness' (1 Enoch 61^{11}), the 'spirit of power' (1 Enoch 61^{11}), the 'spirit of understanding' (Test. Levi 2^3, 18^7), the 'spirit of

---

[13] So, spirit of filthy lucre (Test. Judah 16^1), envy (Test. Simeon, 3^1, 4^7), fighting (Test. Reuben 3^4), jealousy (Test. Judah 13^3), lust (Test. Judah 16^1), pride (Test. Reuben 3^5), vainglory (Test. Dan. 1^6), etc.
[14] op. cit., p. 203.

truth' (Test. Judah 20^{1,5}), the 'spirit of righteousness' (1 Enoch 62^2).

With reference to this 'spirit-concept' development we can refer to one of the most recent manuscripts of the lately discovered Dead Sea Scrolls[15] to be translated, namely, the *Manual of Discipline*. This *Manual* records interesting teaching of a body known as the Damascus Community which was a deeply religious and widely influential movement in Judaism during the last two centuries B.C.[16]

Amongst other details this document offers interesting teaching which is relevant to our present discussion. It is suggested that there are two spirits which strive for the conquest of a man's life. These spirits are the 'spirit of perversion' and the 'spirit of truth' (3^{17}–4^1).[17] The spirit of truth brings enlightenment, gives a man discernment for the way of righteousness, and causes 'his heart to tremble with the judgements of God', brings humility, slowness to anger, a great compassion and eternal goodness, is the giver of 'understanding and insight and mighty wisdom . . .'. This spirit brings 'knowledge and zeal for righteousness and holy purposes' and a loathing for all that is evil and impure. 'Walking by the counsels of the spirit' means receiving healing, abundant peace, everlasting blessings and eternal rejoicing in the victorious life of eternity and a crown of glory (4$^{2-8}$).

On the other hand, the spirit of perversion brings greediness, 'indolence of the hands in the service of righteousness, weakness and falsehood, pride and haughtiness of heart, lying and deceit, cruelty . . . quick temper . . . proud jealousy . . . loathsome works . . . blindness of eyes and dullness of ears . . . and hardening the heart to walk in all the ways of darkness and crafty thought'. The result of a life so possessed by evil brings affliction, eternal ruin and perpetual disgrace and final destruction 'in the fires of the dark regions' (4$^{9-14}$).

Such is the battle that is waged in the life of a man. There follows a concept of deliverance that resembles later Christian thought, for the *Manual* declares that the conflict will be ultimately resolved by the intervention of God in the lives of those

---

[15] cf. A. Dupont-Sommer, *The Dead Sea Scrolls*, pp. 9ff.; H. H. Rowley, *The Zadokite Fragments and the Dead Sea Scrolls*, p. 3, n. 6.

[16] Dupont-Sommer, op. cit., pp. 99f.

[17] Translation of the *Manual of Discipline* in the *Bulletin of the American Schools of Oriental Research*, Supplementary Studies, 10–12 (January 1951), by W. H. Brownlee.

who are willing to be His. 'God will purge by His truth all the deeds of men . . . to cleanse him through a Holy Spirit from all wicked practice . . . to give the upright insight into the knowledge of the Most High . . . to give a perfect way of understanding' (4^{20-7}).

From the above discussion we can conclude that the Spirit's presence was ultimately found in activities and qualities which could only be derived from God Himself. Baser activities could only have their origin in base and evil sources—the demons.

Therefore, though there are certain similarities between the two kinds of spirit experience, there are vital differences. The activities of the demons are always *injurious* to human life, having terrible and disastrous effects in personal and social life. Possession by the Spirit, however, is an experience which enhances personality and brings untold blessing to society. Whilst demon-possession disintegrates personality, the Spirit's indwelling unifies human life. Demon-possession is unclean and unholy; holiness belongs to the experience of the Spirit. The demons are hostile to the rule of God; the Spirit, however, is recognized as the active power in God's Kingdom. Whilst demons induce terror, delusion and insanity, those possessed by the Spirit have joy, peace, patience and confidence. Demon-possession forces its victim away from God into dark and tragic isolation, but those who experience possession by the Spirit are brought near to God and derive from Him new character and their words and lives henceforth reveal that they are 'of the Spirit'.[18]

Dr James S. Stewart[19] has done incalculable service to the thought of the Church by reminding theologians that to be influenced by those who would 'banish the demonic' from our theological concept has had a detrimental effect. Sin is an 'outside force' that 'gets hold of a man' and not just a predicament of life which can be dealt with under some such formula as 'the divided self'. The 'elimination of the dimension of the demonic', concludes Dr Stewart, means that 'We have lost the emphasis that what is really at issue in the age-long tragic dilemma of Romans 7 . . . is not a higher self or lower self, . . . what is at stake is the strengthening or the weakening of the spirit forces of evil that are out to destroy the Kingdom of Christ'.[20] 'Our

---

[18] cf. Hopwood, op. cit., p. 205.
[19] *A Faith to Proclaim*, p. 76. See also C. Anderson Scott, *Christianity according to St Paul*, pp. 28ff.; also, Herbert Butterfield, *Christianity in European History*, p. 57.
[20] op. cit., p. 78.

wrestling is not against flesh and blood' (Ephesians 6^{12}) but against a ruthless invisible realm that would wreck the rule of Christ. Such a sinister foe that completely shatters life can only be met and conquered by 'the fire of the divine'.[21] The living flame causes men to tremble 'and devils fear and fly'.

[21] op. cit., p. 103.

SECTION THREE

Significance of the Abnormal and Supernormal Phenomena in relation to Certain New Testament and Early Church Problems

(a) Pentecost
(b) Corinthian Glossolalia
(c) Montanism

CHAPTER EIGHT

The Spirit on the Day of Pentecost

THE PICTURE of the Day of Pentecost is of a company of enthusiastic and expectant men and women who gathered in Jerusalem in great anticipation. They gave themselves up to prayer, meditation, and worship. Then, as they were gathered together with perfect oneness of heart there came 'a sound as of the rushing of a mighty wind, and it filled all the house where they were sitting. And there appeared unto them tongues parting asunder, like as of fire; and it sat upon each one of them . . .' (Acts $2^{2f.}$). Luke's words are evidently carefully chosen, and are the words of one who is convinced that there is a historical basis for a spiritual experience. The abnormal phenomena might very well be vision, but not visionary. An unspiritual bystander would have had no perception of them, and had he been at the prayer-meeting earlier he might have shaken his head and raised his eyebrows, but unbelief does not turn history into legend. The concrete imagery of the Day of Pentecost was eminently fitted to suggest the truths needing to be conveyed. The seeming rush of a mighty storm-wind, what better symbol of the רוּחַ could have been mentioned to Jews?

We have observed that for Luke, who edited the report of events which we are now considering, Pentecost was the fulfilment of the prophecies of ancient Israel (cf. Isaiah 32^{15}, 44^3). Some choose to interpret the event as a spiritual revival of the heart (Ezekiel 11^{19}, $36^{26f.}$, 39^{29}), others would say that it was the miracle of the starting of the parousia (Joel 3^{1-5}). There is no doubt that Jesus Himself followed the same line of prophecy (Luke 11^{13}, 24^{49}; John 14^{16}, 15^{26}, 16^{7-14}). The report in Acts 2 and the following chapters confirms the view that when the first Christian community was built up, the coming of the Spirit became reality in history. It meant the desired fulfilment and a powerful creative beginning at the same time. The miracle was left in mystical vagueness. Something indescribable happens to the disciples 'like a storm wind' and 'like cloven tongues of fire'—concrete images demonstrating the descent of the Spirit seemed quite relevant to the facts. We have seen that רוּחַ or πνεῦμα was associated with power in the storm-wind, so that symbol was most naturally used in the Pentecostal report. It is also an ancient and obvious idea that spirit and fire belong together. We are told of rabbis who were surrounded by flames when engaged in discussing the Holy Scriptures.

One of the celebrities of Jerusalem had invited all the other celebrities of Jerusalem to a feast on the day of his son's circumcision. They were seated in one room, among them being the Rabbi Eliezer and Rabbi Jehoshua. After having dined, the party was going to clap hands and to dance. Rabbi Eliezer spoke to Rabbi Jehoshua: 'While those are engaged in their way (to their hearts' content) let us be engaged in our own way.' So they studied the words of the *Torah*. From the *Torah* they turned to the Prophets and from the Prophets to the *Hagiographa*. Then fire came down suddenly from heaven and encircled them. The host cried: 'Sirs, do you want to burn my house?' They answered: 'Far be it from us! We were only seated and studying the words of the *Torah*. From the *Torah* we turned to the Prophets, and from the Prophets to the *Hagiographa*, and the words were as joyful as when they were spoken on Mount Sinai, for originally they burned with fire' (cf. Deuteronomy 4[11]).

Or again, it is told that Ben Azzai sat and lectured in public encircled by fire. His disciples went and told Rabbi Aqiba: 'Rabbi ben Azzai sits and is lecturing encircled by fire.' Rabbi Aqiba went and asked Rabbi b. Azzai: 'I was told you were lecturing encircled by fire?' He answered: 'Yes, sir.' Rabbi Aqiba said: 'Perhaps you were considering the secrets of the *Merkaba?*' He answered: 'No, sir, but I was studying the words of the *Torah* (to understand these words) and from the *Torah* I went to the Prophets and from the Prophets to the *Hagiographa*, and the words were as joyful as they were when they were given on Mount Sinai and they were as lovely (clear, intelligible) as when given for the first time, for were they not given by fire originally?' (cf. Deuteronomy 4[11]; T.B. *Chagigah*, 2.77a. 43). Rabbi Abbahu sat and was lecturing when he was encircled by fire. He asked: 'Did I not string the words together correctly?' Once Rabbi Jochanan b. Zakkai travelled. He rode on an ass. Rabbi Eliazar b. Arakh walked behind him and spoke to him: 'Rabbi, teach me a chapter from the

Merkaba.' He answered: 'Have not our wise men taught that one must not lecture about the *Merkaba* except if the hearer is a learned man having an independent judgement?' Then the other said: 'Rabbi, allow me to speak about it.' He answered: 'Go on.' When Rabbi Eliazar b. Arakh began to explain the *Merkaba,* Rabbi Jochanan b. Zakkai dismounted and spoke: 'It is not right for me to hear about the glory of my creator riding on an ass.' They walked and, sitting under a tree, they were encircled by fire falling from heaven, and the angels were dancing before them as the wedding guests are joyful with the bridegroom. Then an angel answered out of the fire and spoke: 'As thou hast expounded Eliazar b. Arakh, so it is, concerning the *Merkaba.*' At once all the trees opened their mouths and spoke a psalm (cf. Psalm 96[12]: 'Then shall all the trees of the wood rejoice'). Parallels are T.B. *Chagigah* 14 and T.B. *Sukkah* 28. About Jonathan ben Uzziel, a contemporary of Jesus, it is told that all the birds flying above his head were burned when he was studying the *Torah* (i.e. by the fire encircling him).[1]

In the ecstasies of Dionysus cults, flames were seen around the heads. The fiery spirit is important in the Stoic conception of God. In the Mithras liturgy the partakers of the rite have to adore God with fire and spirit, whom they call the 'fire-ruling', the 'fire-breathing', the 'lucid' spirit. According to certain tradition, John the Baptist opposed the baptism with the Holy Ghost by his own form of baptism with water.[2]

The gift of the Spirit with fire is given now at Pentecost, when tongues, like tongues of fire, appear to the disciples and something miraculous overcomes them. The Spirit overcomes them. The tongues demonstrate the same thing as the dove descending on Jesus at His baptism for those who are there at the time. When the possessed group move out into the street, they begin to speak in such a manner that the multitude around is amazed, and foreigners hear the possessed ones speak in their own language. As the narrative stands, we are given the impression that these possessed men speak in foreign languages and dialects. Luke explains this phenomenon in a very clear and unmistakable way. A miracle has happened. Luke says that the disciples, who are all natives of Galilee,

---

[1] Strack and Billerbeck, Komm. *Johannes und die Apostelgeschichte,* pp. 602f. See Rabbinic citations collected by W. D. Davies, *Paul and Rabbinic Judaism,* pp. 183f.

[2] H. W. Beyer, *Apostelgeschichte, Das Neue Testament Deutsch,* II.8.

suddenly are able to speak in such a language or languages that all the other Jews who are natives of countries all over the world imagine they are hearing the language of their own countries.

Now there is no doubt that on this Day of Pentecost, something powerful, 'other-than-human', united a cowardly, cowering group of despairing individuals and shot them into a pagan, hostile world as crusading champions. Yet it is the episode of glossolalia on the Day of Pentecost which presents the difficulty. As we have remarked, Luke regarded this glossolalia as speech in a foreign language, but when we compare this report with St Paul's account of glossolalia at Corinth, we find that there is no mention of foreign languages at Corinth. So the question to which some answer must be given is concerning the glossolalia at Pentecost.

Did the glossolalia at Pentecost mean speech in foreign language? What really happened at Pentecost?

Some might read the story and on the face of it dismiss it as legend, but we have seen reason to believe that it preserves the Church's memory of a real occasion, and E. F. Scott says: 'It is possible that even the wind and the appearances of flame are something more than fanciful additions.'[3] However, if Luke intends by the phrase ἑτέραις γλώσσαις, 'foreign tongues', it would appear that he has been under a misapprehension about the event.

In the first place, these opening verses of the narrative in Acts appear to form a separate fragment, to which the author of Acts has appended his story.[4] When they are examined closely, they connect in a loose and awkward manner with the section that follows, and have to be considered apart from it. Secondly, when Peter boldly stands up later and preaches to the bewildered multitude, it is significant that he never suggests directly or indirectly that the noises heard were real languages, although this has previously been emphasized as the outstanding fact in the miracle. What Peter does emphasize is that the old Hebrew power of prophetic consciousness and possession has been reborn and the Spirit has been given again and is available for all. This leads us to point out, in the third place, that the whole point of Peter's speech here and in subsequent speeches is just to emphasize that fact mentioned above—that here is the beginning of a new revival of prophecy. The Spirit

[3] *The Spirit in the New Testament*, p. 94. [4] ibid., pp. 94f.

of the past is reborn; in a number of details, by miracles of healing, by visions, by clairvoyance, etc., this shows itself. In the Christian community is born a new prophetic consciousness—and this consciousness is always linked with the prophetic consciousness of the past. All the associations of that old prophetic consciousness are found in the new community.

Now the gift of speaking in a foreign language was never once associated with the prophetic consciousness and the suggestion that this is a new gift to the prophets of the Christian community seems an intrusion. A fourth consideration is that the 'list of nations' represented as hearing their language is very inadequate. Almost every nation represented by that list would have been conversant with the Greek language or Aramaic—in other words, speaking their own languages and dialects, the disciples would have been understood by any of the 'foreigners'. An ingenious author wishing to prove the miracle of the foreign languages would have to compile a far more extensive list of nations. A fifth point to bear in mind is that if foreign languages were spoken, this is the one and only occasion on which such a gift was given—and why?—for they were not necessary to edify people represented by the reported list. Moreover, the foreign languages were never given to aid the later missionary crusade of the Church. Christian missionaries, from the moment Paul and Barnabas were separated until the most recent men and women sailed to West Africa, have all had to learn with tired brain and splitting head the language of their field. A gift so much emphasized as in this Lucan report would surely have been a gift graciously bestowed upon all crusading champions of the Faith. The sixth consideration is that only certain hearers heard sounds like their own language—others came along, listened, and they only heard babbling that reminded them of the behaviour and disjointed, uncontrolled talk of a crowd of drunken people. In face of the evidence, they assumed that the disciples were the worse for drink. In other words, some understood, others did not understand; some could interpret the disciples' language—others were not able to do so. This has led scholars to suggest that if there were a miracle of speech, there was also a miracle of hearing, enabling some of the crowd to 'hear' and understand their own language, whilst others were outside the influence of the miracle, since they were not able to 'hear' or 'pick up' their particular language. The last point in this connexion is one mentioned above, viz: the conflict between this and Paul's account of glossolalia.

In this story of Acts, by γλώσσαις λαλεῖν is clearly intended 'speaking in a foreign language', ἑτέραις being used later. However, when we turn to Paul's account (1 Corinthians 12, 14), by no amount of forcing or conjecture can γλώσσαις λαλεῖν be made to have the above connotation. Luke and Paul were companions in travel and in thought, and there is little doubt that Luke would be aware of Paul's words to the Corinthian Church on this particular question—it is strange that when he has opportunity to give a report of such events he should interpret things so differently.

Weinel explains the difference in this manner. In post-apostolic times, speaking with tongues was no longer practised. Within the Church, Paul's influence and the natural necessity of ecclesiastical order had reduced and finally extinguished glossolalia. Because glossolalia had fallen into disrepute in this fashion, the author of Acts changed 'speaking with tongues' into 'speaking in foreign languages', although his source explained the miracle of Pentecost differently. In Acts 2, the verses 1–4 (without ἑτέραις), verses 5 and 6a, 12–14, are to be attributed to the original source; verse 7 is a clear parallel to verse 12, and verses 5ff. are the introduction to verse 7.[5] In the other reports of glossolalia in Acts (cf. 10[46], 19[6]) there is every similarity with the Pauline reports. This source would then read as follows:

καὶ ἐν τῷ συμπληροῦσθαι τὴν ἡμέραν τῆς πεντηκοστῆς ἦσαν ἅπαντες ὁμοθυμαδὸν ἐπὶ τὸ αὐτό· καὶ ἐγένετο ἄφνω ἐκ τοῦ οὐρανοῦ ἦχος ὥσπερ φερομένης πνοῆς βιαίας ·καὶ ἐπλήρωσαν ὅλον τὸν οἶκον οὗ ἦσαν καθήμενοι, καὶ ὤφθησαν αὐτοῖς διαμεριζόμεναι γλῶσσαι ὡσεὶ πυρός, καὶ ἐκάθισεν ἐφ᾿ ἕνα ἕκαστον αὐτῶν, καὶ ἐπλήσθησαν πάντες πνεύματος ʿΑγίου, καὶ ἤρξαντο λαλεῖν γλώσσαις καθὼς τὸ πνεῦμα ἐδίδου αὐτοῖς ἀποφθέγγεσθαι· ῏Ησαν δὲ εἰς ʿΙερουσαλὴμ κατοικοῦντες ᾿Ιουδαῖοι, ἄνδρες εὐλαβεῖς ἀπὸ παντὸς ἔθνους τῶν ὑπὸ τὸν οὐρανόν γενομένης δὲ τῆς φωνῆς ταύτης συνῆλθεν τὸ πλῆθος καὶ συνεχύθη ἐξίσταντο δὲ πάντες καὶ διηποροῦντο, ἄλλος πρὸς ἄλλον λέγοντες, Τί θέλει τοῦτο εἶναι; ἕτεροι δὲ χλευάζοντες ἔλεγον ὅτι γλεύκους μεμεστωμένοι εἰσί. . . .

Dr H. W. Beyer adopts the explanation that the author of Acts may have known two different reports about the happen-

[5] *Die Wirkungen des Geistes und der Geister*, pp. 74f.

ings at Pentecost.[6] The first story told of the miraculous effect of speaking with tongues—in Paul's use of the phrase. The second story deals with the miracle enabling the disciples to speak to all the peoples of the earth in their own languages; this same source reports about the impression made by the first speaking with tongues: '... here the enthusiasm, the impetuous emotion of this first Church expressing itself by talking with a strange speech and even more by the strength of love and faithful readiness of God, happening but once, which has become a reality in history and was so indissolubly connected with the prophecies of the Old Testament and the life and word of Jesus Himself.' But the story of Pentecost has a deeper meaning by the amalgamation with a second report. The stammering praying by talking with tongues is an experience of the Spirit which closely unites the individual with God. Now this speaking in other languages is supposed to express how the power of the Spirit will give a world-wide efficiency from mouth to mouth.

Professor Wilhelm Michaëlis takes the report of the Pentecost incident as it stands, but does not see in it any contradiction with the Pauline description.[7] The descent of the Spirit is no outward event, but 'the acoustic and optical impression of the simultaneous but nevertheless personally felt certainty of the Holy Spirit. We are told of wind and fiery tongues only by way of comparison, and within this comparison the author speaks of tongues, not of fire, but of cloven tongues like as of fire'. It is not asserted that these tongues had replaced the tongues in the mouths. Luke does *not* want to describe a miracle of language, but thinks of the gift of the Spirit in general without the restriction of speaking with tongues. Paul makes use of the same expression which Luke uses for the same phenomena. Michaëlis admits, however, 'of course the Greek word γλῶσσα may mean language . . . but here no speaking in foreign languages unknown to the speakers is meant'. The incident is the phenomenon of speaking in rapture, an ecstasy only intelligible by a special gift of the Spirit; no different languages were spoken. 'Nearly all of the persons present must have spoken and understood universal Greek. . . . The people understood the speaking with tongues, though it was genuinely unintelligible—they understood because they too had been filled with the Spirit and had received the gift of understanding.

[6] op. cit., II.15.   [7] ibid., II.11-12.

... It was a mass ecstasy in which most of the hearers present were involved. ...' The hearers, however, would not know that they were witnesses of the descent of the Holy Spirit and that they were included in this event. That was why, says Michaëlis, they had to ask questions. 'But there is no reason to suppose that Luke has mistaken this event as a miracle of language ... and that Judea is mentioned in the catalogues of nations is further proof that no miracle of language is described.' So Pentecost is the birthday of a mission, and the power of that mission is the power of the Spirit. There is no claim for the one Gospel to be preached to mankind in many languages—but that this Gospel is a gift for all peoples and that the Spirit is able to overcome all separating and dividing differences. 'Not a miracle of languages, but the speaking through the inspiration of the Holy Spirit, the telling of God's marvellous deeds, will overcome the Babylonian confusion; not one language, but one spirit. ...' Professor Michaëlis has been very kind to the author of Acts, but facts seem to point the other way; it seems that Luke, or a later editor[8] *intended* something different whilst what actually happened was just what Professor Michaëlis suggests.

In contrast to these expositions of the phenomena of Pentecost, it has been surmised that certain Old Testament and Jewish parallels were present in the mind of the writer of Acts. The first parallel is that of the Tower of Babel, where the phenomena were the reverse of Pentecost: 'The men of "the beginning" had one speech, intelligible not only to all men, but even to all animals—cf. Philo, *De confus. ling.*, 3, p. 405: "And there is also another story akin to this, related by the devisers of fables, concerning the sameness of language existing among animals: for they say that formerly, all the animals in the world, whether land animals, or aquatic ones, or winged ones, had but one language ..."—and cf. also Josephus, *Antiq.*, i.1.4: "Now God commanded Adam and his wife to eat all of the other plants, but to abstain from the tree of knowledge. ... But as all living creatures had one language at that time, the serpent, who then lived together with Adam and his wife spoke ..." Owing to their sin this primitive language was "confounded"; that of all animals at the fall, that of men at the Tower of Babel, but at "the End" the redeemed will again have but one speech.'[9]

[8] See Weinel, op. cit., pp. 74f.   [9] Lake, *Beginnings of Christianity*, V.114ff.

THE SPIRIT ON THE DAY OF PENTECOST 87

A second parallel is another Jewish legend known to us from Philo in *De Decal.* ix–xi.32–49. This is a story of the delivering of the Law on Sinai. God does not speak there like a human being, but on His command a sound pierces the air. It is a clear and distinct sound, sound out of which a language is formed. The whole atmosphere is full of the miraculous. There are claps of thunder much louder than human ears can stand; the bright shining of flashes of lightning; the sound of an invisible trumpet to be heard from a very great distance; a moving cloud like a column with its base on the ground, but extending to great heights; a floating, heavenly fire overlapping all things in dense smoke. Then a voice came out of the midst of the fire descending from heaven and all the people were filled with awful terror. The flame was changed into a language known to all the hearers, the spoken word sounded so clear that it seemed visible rather than audible.

Another parallel[10] is from the theologies of the rabbis concerning the giving of the Law on Sinai. Here the voice of God was divided into seventy voices representing the seventy languages of mankind. 'Although the ten Commandments were promulgated with a single sound, it says, "All people heard the voices"; it follows then that when the voice went forth it was divided into seven voices and then went into seventy tongues, and every people received the law in their own language' (*Midrash Tanhuma* 26c.) (*Schab.* 88). Rabbi Jochanan wrote: 'What means Psalm 68[11]: "The Lord gave the word. Great was the company of those that published it."? Every word going out from God's mouth (on the occasion of the law-giving on Mount Sinai) was divided into seventy tongues (languages) so that each people could hear the divine commandments in its own language.' Or a passage from the school of Rabbi Ishmael: 'It is written, Jeremiah 23[29]: "Is not my word like a fire," saith the Lord, "and like a hammer that breaketh the rock in pieces?" The hammer produces many sparks. Likewise the word going out from God's mouth was divided into seventy tongues. It is written, Deuteronomy 5[22]: "These words the Lord spake unto all your assembly . . . with a great voice, and he added no more"' (*Midr*: with a voice which never ceased). Billerbeck says that according to certain Midrashic comments, the seven voices are derived from the sevenfold use of the word קול in the narrative of the law-giving in Exodus, viz. 19[16]

[10] Lake, *Beginnings of Christianity*, V.116.

(קוֹל used twice), 19^{19} (twice), 20^{18} (twice), and 24^{3}.[11] Rabbi Tanhuma says of this event: 'The voice went out with a double effect. It killed people because they did not accept the *Torah*, but it gave life to the Israelites, because they accepted the *Torah*. So Moses told them at the end of the forty years: (Deuteronomy 5^{24}) "Behold, the Lord our God hath showed us this glory and His greatness and we have heard His voice out of the midst of the fire," and 5^{26}: "For who is there of all flesh that hath heard the voice of the living God speaking out of the midst of the fire as we have and liveth? You have heard His voice and you are living, but the peoples of the world hearing this voice have died."[12] Lake suggests that few of these statements in Rabbinic literature can be proved to be as early as Acts.[13]

A third parallel is Isaiah 28$^{11f.}$, which is quoted by Paul in 1 Corinthians 14^{21}: 'For with stammering lips and another tongue will he speak to this people . . . yet they would not hear.' Lake remarks that this parallel is much more striking if we accept the text omitting Jews at the beginning of the story and suppose that Luke regarded the preaching at Pentecost as the beginning of the mission to the Gentiles; the foreigners understood what was said, each man hearing the apostles in his own language, but it was unintelligible to the Jews, who thought the speakers drunk.[14]

It is quite possible that many of these 'parallels' would be known to Luke, and reminiscences of this kind would be natural—especially so if the giving of the law, as some evidence would lead us to believe, was commemorated in the feast of Pentecost. It would be natural for the writer to describe the birth of the new Israel in terms suggested by the anniversary of the ancient covenant. Yet there is no need to assume this background for the story. It may be that Luke's love of symbolism is evident here. In his Gospel he changes the true order of the narrative in order to foreshadow, in the rejection of Jesus of Nazareth, the future refusal of his message by his own people. In like manner, he may desire a typical frontispiece for his history of the Christian mission, and obtains it by allowing his imagination to play on the story of Pentecost on that first day of the Church. All the nations which were hereafter to be gathered into the Kingdom of God were represented at Jeru-

---

[11] Strack and Billerbeck, op. cit., II.604f.   [12] ibid., p. 605.
[13] Lake, op. cit., V.116.   [14] ibid., V.115.

salem, and the disciples were given power to address the Gospel to each of them in its own tongue.[15]

Lake gives a theory of a 'source for Acts 2'.[16] Probably Luke was dealing with a written source which did not say anything about speaking in foreign languages, but gave an extraordinary description of glossolalia, such as Paul describes. He himself had not been present at scenes where glossolalia was to be observed, but he knew that it had been a common experience of the Early Church. He wrote a report, but he was influenced by a natural but wrong etymology and also by the Old Testament and Jewish parallels (discussed above), hence he explained glossolalia as speaking in foreign languages and rewrote the story so as to bring out his own interpretation. Lake suggests that this hypothesis can be supported on the following grounds:

(a) The inconsistency with the Pauline description of glossolalia, and

(b) Inconsistencies in the narrative itself.

When he is dealing with (a), Lake remarks that this inconsistency can easily be exaggerated. It is often overlooked that Paul speaks not merely of glossolalia but also of a corresponding gift of the Spirit which enables men to understand glossolalia. When brethren were sometimes seized with an attack of ecstatic speech which was entirely unintelligible to most of the congregation—this was glossolalia. Yet there were always a few in the congregation who would believe that they did understand—to them the glossolalia was not unintelligible. In the same way, Luke may mean that on the Day of Pentecost, when the Christians were gifted with glossolalia some of the pious visitors were also gifted with the power of interpreting the speech which they identified with their own dialects, while the rest were not so inspired, and needed Peter's speech in order to explain the situation. Lake concludes: 'Interpreted on these lines there is nothing in the narrative essentially inconsistent with Paul's statements.' It seems that it is intrinsically improbable that Luke as a companion of Paul should have written in unredeemed contradiction to Pauline teaching. Even if—as is probable—he had never read 1 Corinthians, he could hardly have been ignorant of Paul's teaching, and it is important to note that the story as it stands can well be a redaction of an earlier document, made by a member of the

[15] E. F. Scott, op. cit., p. 96.   [16] op. cit., V.117–19.

Pauline School who did not fully understand it, but who was imbued with the Pauline distrust of unintelligible glossolalia.

We have already mentioned a number of the inconsistencies within the narrative itself, viz. the inadequate catalogue of nations; the miracle of hearing; the anti-climax of Peter's speech. Lake concludes this section dealing with (*b*): '. . . it is not inconceivable that Luke believed that glossolalia was speaking in languages which some pious people could understand though ordinary men could not, and therefore inserted "other" before "tongues", and added the story of the "pious" visitors. In this way he produced the double statement of their astonishment in verses 7 and 12, and forgot to insert any reference to this story into the speech of Peter. . . . Thus . . . it seems that there is not enough evidence to make the hypothesis certain, though it is not impossible or even improbable. Incidentally it may be noted that if it be true it indicates that the speech of Peter was in Luke's source, and was not composed by him; for had he composed it, he would surely have dealt with the story of the pious Jews who understood the apostles.'

The following is a summary of Lake's conclusion on the historical value of the narrative under consideration. He takes the general standard of probability as a guide, but remarks that there are certain features in the account of the Day of Pentecost which do not seem to be historical:

'(*a*) It is unlikely that any body of men witnessing the phenomena described ever made a speech in which they gave a complete catalogue of the nations from which they had been taken.

'(*b*) It is unlikely that men who were not members of the Christian community thought that they were capable of understanding Christians who were speaking with tongues. The same emotional circumstances which lead one man in any given congregation to speak with tongues may conceivably lead another in the same congregation to think that he understands him, but this would not apply to those outside the group.

'(*c*) Just as it is extremely likely that the Day of Pentecost was marked by the first instance of glossolalia in the Christian community, it is extremely unlikely that this took the form of speaking in foreign languages. The tradition of the foreign languages is the attempt to explain the glossolalia by a friendly author, separated by time from the actual event, just as the charge of drunkenness was the attempt of unfriendly observers, separated by lack of sympathy. Quite possibly the form of the Lucan narrative was partly brought about by the desire to refute damaging accusations. The presence of the foreigners may be merely complementary to that of the miracle of languages, and designed to support it. This would be by no means a unique instance of an improbable imaginary incident being supported by an equally imaginary but slightly less improbable collection of witnesses. But this view is not necessary, and it is by no means impossible that the first notable increase in the numbers of the Christian community was really the result of the inspired preaching of the Day of Pentecost, and was due to the effect of the glossolalia on those who listened.'

After allowing to these points as much or as little weight as may seem necessary, Lake observes that one positive conclusion stands out. At the beginning of its history the apostolic circle in Jerusalem underwent a deeply moving psychological experience. It was of the nature which to that and many later generations was known as 'inspiration'. They had made no claim to inspiration during Christ's life, but did so almost immediately afterwards. Luke may have misinterpreted the facts when he makes the polygot witnesses of the Pentecost abnormalities say that they were hearing 'every man his own language' spoken. Some would make the ingenuous and spiritual suggestion that there is an underlying truth conveyed in such an impression. It has been suggested that Luke is speaking metaphorically, and that a crowd did hear the 'wonders of God' noised abroad in a manner which they could understand—though not through the medium of their own language. John Woolman once spoke to Indians, and finding the interpreters of little use spoke in English. The result was, in his own words: 'I believe the Holy Ghost was wrought on some hearts to edification where all words were not understood.' In so far as the Spirit-possessed preacher was understood, it may have seemed that he spoke in their own language. A clearer instance is cited by C. Anderson Scott,[17] in reference to an ecumenical conference of the Salvation Army, 'at which were present representatives of nations even more numerous and more heterogeneous than those tabulated in Acts 2'. A report of one of the meetings contains the following striking sentence: 'Each time the theme

[17] Art. 'What Happened at Pentecost?' (in *The Spirit*, edited by B. H. Streeter), pp. 128f.

was touched upon, it brought forth from the pent-up feelings of the vast assembly a sort of half-sigh of appreciation; yet many of the audience knew no English, but they felt that the one great truth to them was being announced at this particular moment. Indians, Chinese, Canadians, inhabitants of Peru, Swedes, etc., all of them together gave the deep emotional sigh.' Professor Scott goes on to say that 'it would not be difficult to believe that when the speaker on that occasion had finished, representatives of these various races would be found saying: "We heard him speaking in our own tongue the mighty works of God." '

I recall to mind an incident related some years ago by the late Rev. J. Sadler Reece, then of the Stoke-on-Trent Methodist Mission. He told how, as a young man, he had been present at some of the meetings of the Welsh Revival under Evan Roberts. Sadler Reece could not speak Welsh, but he endeavoured to take part in the great meetings though they were being conducted in Welsh—Welsh singing and Welsh preaching. He recalled moving with them as they did street marches before the evening meetings. Without words he caught the strain of their revival songs. The march over, they went into a place of prayer, and with spirits aglow with the singing and with a hurting passion and concern for those who were 'lost', they literally groaned in prayer. Then came the next meeting with its fiery eloquence and revival preaching. The amazing testimony of Sadler Reece was that, though he knew not the language, he knew what they were talking about, he had felt the same thrill in song, he was moved with a similar power in prayer, and in the revival meeting was carried away by the same fervour and felt that in his own tongue he had heard of the mighty words of God. Dr Dawson Walker cites similar instances. In the same Welsh Revival, young Welsh people, normally speaking English because they knew little or no Welsh, when under the influence of the revival they took part in public prayer, sometimes used not the familiar English but the merely partially known Welsh, speaking it too with seeming ease and correctness, except that the Welsh bore the stamp of an English accent.[18] The account of another unique happening is given by Dr J. A. Findlay.[19] He states that he has heard a Durham miner, who in ordinary conversation could not put together a sentence that Dr Findlay could understand

[18] *The Gift of Tongues*, pp. 56f.   [19] *Commentary, Acts*, p. 66.

until he was familiar with his dialect, pour forth in a prayer-meeting a flood of beautiful English, completely free from obscurities of pronunciation or faults of grammar, nor was he quoting either Bible or hymn-book during the greater part of his prayer. The man was quite sure that this was the result of real inspiration, and was a modern parallel to what happened at Pentecost.

There are those who suggest that Luke was giving a report of an event similar to those above—that the onlookers at Pentecost may have so caught the spiritual strains of the ecstasy of speaking with tongues that it seemed to everyone that the disciples were speaking in several languages. However, there are great differences; the audience of the ecumenical conference in Scott's account was *en rapport* with the theme of the speaker; Sadler Reece was likewise 'one' in mind and heart with the revivalists. At Pentecost, on the other hand, we have a surprised body of polyglot people who came across the believers speaking in the languages represented by the onlookers, as Luke reports it. This vital distinction tells against this suggested interpretation, for there was no psychological unity of experience, and no necessary spiritual sympathy between the pilgrims and the disciples.

Bearing in mind, therefore, the conclusions mentioned in the rather extensive survey outlined above, we would suggest that it is fairly certain that the 'tongues' of Pentecost were not foreign languages. We have seen that such a miracle would in any case have been unnecessary, since all the races enumerated spoke Greek, yet apart from this, the other New Testament references to glossolalia make it abundantly clear that they were not in the proper sense languages. On the other hand, we must admit that the writer of the record in Acts himself concludes that foreign languages have been spoken. This is clearly *not* due to ignorance of the true nature of glossolalia. In later parts of the book the author makes occasional reference to 'tongues' without any indication that he regards such speech as a foreign language (Acts 10^{46}, 19^6). We have no definite means of knowing why in this report foreign languages are suggested. It may indeed be that Luke is influenced by Jewish and Old Testament parallels, or that he is speaking metaphorically. It may be conjectured that while fully aware that tongues were unintelligible, he believed, in common with many of his contemporaries, that they were real languages. 'Luke apparently believes that the sounds uttered in glossolalia are not merely arbitrary. To be sure, they have no meaning to the casual hearer, but if an audience could be selected from all the races of the earth, there would be some who would be able to recognize their own language.'[20] In the story of Pentecost this is made to happen. Representatives of all nations are gathered at Jerusalem, and in that polyglot assembly the 'tongues' which are often put down to mere raving are discerned in their true character. Each form of glossolalia is a language to those who are qualified to understand it. Broad considerations would seem to show, therefore, that whatever additional element might have belonged to it, the Pentecostal phenomenon was akin to the glossolalia at Corinth and elsewhere, in that it was psychologically a disturbance of the normal consciousness due to the up-rushing of a mighty wave of emotion, the result being that men broke out into ecstatic and almost hysterical utterance.

Now before we close this discussion of happenings on the day of Pentecost, it might be opportune to conclude with remarks about the significance of the events on this day to the Christian community. Pentecost is regarded as inaugurating a new era which Christian thinkers have sometimes described as 'the dispensation of the Spirit'. God, who had initiated one stage of His redemption work by sending forth 'His Son', then inaugurated the final one by sending forth 'the Spirit of His Son' (Galatians 4[4ff.]). This sharp distinction making Pentecost into a sort of spiritual watershed, parting all that went before from all that followed after, might demand some explanation. In what sense was the Spirit operative in the world at and after Pentecost as He was not before?

From our previous reading in Section Two above, we cannot wholly exclude the activity of the Spirit from the earlier epoch. The Spirit was active in the world—active in the created world and active in men, but only active in human personality as men became capable of the Spirit's invasion. One might say that the Spirit would not force any doors; the demons did that. Pentecost marked no new way in the divine method of breaking through into human life. The power increased because there was a greater company of men and women prepared to

[20] E. F. Scott, op. cit., p. 98.

fulfil certain conditions, and throwing all selfish interests to the winds, would allow themselves to be swept anywhere by the new inrush of power. So Pentecost witnessed the impressive manifestation of a power which had already come.

Throughout Acts there is a remarkable feature in the book—the prominence of this divine over the human element in life and work. The book begins with the story of the invasion of human personality by the Spirit, and the rest of that book tells the thrilling story of what happened when men invaded in that fashion attacked a hostile, pagan world. Whatever else happened, Jesus was an exalted Conqueror. Denney says: 'The whole Pentecostal phenomenon . . . has the character of a testimony to Jesus. . . . The gift and possession of the Spirit is the proof to the world of the exaltation of Jesus. It is His Divine power which is behind this incalculable elevation and reinforcement of the natural life. . . .'[21]

Another point to notice is the prominence given to the day of Pentecost. It is clearly to be regarded as unique, both as the culmination of previous expectation and also as the beginning of the new society. Yet it is true that the closing verses of the second chapter of the Acts, with their picture of the simple, joyful, strenuous life of the newly baptized in the days that followed the Pentecost, reveal even more than the abnormal phenomena of the Pentecost itself, the nature of the Power which had come to dwell with the Church.[22]

What, then, are we to understand as the meaning and significance of this Day of Pentecost to the primitive Christian community?

(*a*) First of all, it was held to be the vindication of Christ to the Jews. It was the demonstration of His character and claim (Acts 2^{22-36}).

(*b*) It was an invasion of power among the disciples. They felt that they had become recipients of something which previously they had not possessed. It may have been, of course, that on this day there was only a conscious reception of a power which had always been in the world and had been operative even within themselves, though in ways too quiet, normal, and undramatic for them to have learnt to recognize it as the power of the Spirit—but the fact is, the difference which this invasion made was seen after Pentecost. They were made capable of

---

[21] Article, 'Holy Spirit' (*H.D.B.*), I.737.
[22] H. B. Swete, *The Holy Spirit in the New Testament*, p. 71.

facing any emergency; the very essence of this invasion by the Spirit meant for them that they could face any situation at any time and be absolutely certain of coming out victoriously. The Peter of the Day of Pentecost is a new man, far other than the Peter of the Passover ... and in courage and general understanding of the new situation Peter was not alone: the whole company of believers was filled with the same Spirit. From that day forward a new strength which was not their own marked all the sayings and deeds of the Apostolic Church. 'It is in this great change of mental and spiritual attitude rather than in the external signs of mind and fire or in strange powers of utterance that we recognize the supreme miracle of Pentecost.'[23]

(c) This day marks the moment when the new community of the Church was constituted. Perhaps some would say literally that the birthday of the Christian Church was that occasion on which the two disciples of John the Baptist heard their master speak and followed Jesus (John 1^{37}), yet the Day of Pentecost may rightly be called the commencement of the Christian Church among the Jews.

(d) Not only was there on this day an invasion of the Spirit into human personality (viz. (b)), but there was an invasion or entrance of the Spirit into all the details of human life. All through His life, and especially in its later stages, Jesus had spoken of a Kingdom and a coming gift, and His followers had been told to wait until they were endued with power from on high (Luke 24^{49}; Acts $1^{4f.}$). On this day they knew the reward of waiting.

This invasion, once begun, continues in the life of the primitive Christian community—there are six further accounts of the gift of the Spirit. On the Day of Pentecost we have the commencement of the Jewish Christian Church (Acts 2); later a special bestowal for testimony (4^{31}); there comes the extension of the Church to the Samaritans by the power of the Spirit (8); there follows the conversion of the Apostle of the Gentiles (9); the extension of the Church to the Gentiles (10); then the special occasion at Ephesus (19). Such is the power manifested after Pentecost; any new departure or policy was right which either was initiated by the Spirit or subsequently endorsed by him.

[23] H. B. Swete, *The Holy Spirit in the New Testament*, p. 76; also J. S. Stewart, *The Gates of New Life*, pp. 99–101.

'The early history of the Church recorded in the Acts is a kind of extended Pentecost. On that day a pellucid spring of new life is seen pouring forth from the mountain side, and the first years of the Church show us the course of the stream, in its primitive freshness and purity, the first effervescence of what can only be described as a *Vita Nuova*, a New Life.'[24]

[24] W. T. Davidson, *The Indwelling Spirit*, p. 81. See also W. H. G. Thomas, *The Holy Spirit of God*, pp. 42ff.

CHAPTER NINE

Corinthian Glossolalia

IN THE previous discussion we have frequently referred to Pauline teaching about glossolalia, either contrasting or comparing his teaching with that expressed in Luke's account of the happenings at Pentecost. Moreover, we have reached the conclusion that the Pentecostal phenomenon was akin to the glossolalia at Corinth and elsewhere. We must now discover, as far as we are able, what exactly Corinthian glossolalia was, why it seemed to manifest itself only at Corinth, i.e. in a problematic form, and, if it came from outside sources, where exactly were those sources.

Whether we are thinking of happenings at Pentecost or events in the 'warm' atmosphere of a Corinthian cottage-meeting we should not overlook the influence of the group when discussing the question of glossolalia. A company of individuals, says P. G. S. Hopwood, under the same religious stress induces an element which is in itself a powerful means of heightening the suggestibility of the whole gathering.[1] Hopwood continues: ..... 'The mutual "continuing instant in prayer" of the believers in the Upper Room reacted on the individuals there. Each took the fire from each; the whole group became religiously and psychologically infected by the experience of the individual members. After their renewed fellowship with Jesus risen from the dead, and sure that He was soon to return, they went back to Jerusalem to await the promise of the Father in the coming of the power which should descend on them. The crisis was at hand. The days went by and every disciple influenced the rest in earnest desire, which increased the more they met and talked about it; they encouraged one another in joyful hope and prayer continually, and everyone was in a state of preparedness and like-mindedness . . . the big thing happened. The clouds of heaven, as it were, burst upon them, mind and spirit received illumination, the limiting inhibitions which bound them . . . were done away as in heart and mind and will the believers were surrendered entirely to

[1] op. cit., p. 162.

the new power that came upon them. The tide of emotion swept to and fro and set up psychological abnormalities which have led some scholars to conclude that these were but accretions, but which were rather the historical mythical indices of a vital religious awakening.'

It may seem that the above paragraph is irrelevant to the present discussion of Corinthian glossolalia. On the contrary, it is very much to the point. Such 'group' gatherings which evidently preceded the Pentecost experience became part of the heritage of every Christian community. It is clear from the subsequent narrative in Acts that after a missioner had toured a district many such groups were organized, friends were invited to attend, the hearth became a holy place, and the table became an altar for the Memorial Meal. Moreover, it seems clear also that these groups were encouraged to expect the same experience as was known on the Day of Pentecost. In other words, the Upper Room meetings before Pentecost became a 'type' for the Church in every place. In this way the greater Church was united by a common hope, a common surrender, and a common experience. The Church in every place met together in groups and found a corporate experience of power. The word 'seek' or 'discover' in relation to the Pentecostal experience has not been used. It does not appear that they 'sought' or had 'retreats' to discover the secret of Pentecost. They *expected* to know the same power, to see the same accompaniments, and they were not disappointed.

We find, therefore, that in the brief pages of the later narrative in the Acts, Pentecost was repeated, and there is no reason to doubt that there were other occasions, unreported, when the expectant people were filled with the Holy Spirit. It would appear that in Palestinian Christianity the group which expected another Pentecost was encouraged, and wherever the Apostles of the first order went they gave this same encouragement. In a similar connexion we may point out that the New Testament gives evidence for the existence of a definite form of ethical instruction or *catechesis* in the early days of the Christian mission. The epistles show common style and form when dealing with similar ethical ideas and problems. The suggestion is that these passages are based upon an accepted pattern of teaching which goes back to a very early period.[2] May it not be

[2] See C. H. Dodd, *Gospel and Law*, pp. 12-22; also Philip Carrington, *The Primitive Christian Catechism*; and E. G. Selwyn, *The First Epistle of St Peter* (Appendix).

that the question asked at Ephesus 'Did ye receive the Holy Spirit when ye believed?' (Acts 19^{12}) was one of the first and most prominent questions asked by the itinerant evangelists as a preliminary to this catechetical teaching? This was crucial for the early Church; wherever the missionaries went—and they went in the power of the Spirit—they expected a similar manifestation to that at Pentecost. The question about receiving the Holy Spirit is reported at this place in Acts because of the amazing admission that here was a Christian community which was subnormal—they did not know about Pentecost, and had not been encouraged to expect a 'local invasion of the Spirit'! This was of all things most disastrous; they were existing at a low level spiritually.

Meyer makes the ingenious suggestion that Paul was ranked an equal apostle by this incident!—that the writer has purposely drawn up the scene which was needed to give the authority of the Spirit to Paul. The writer needed for his purpose a special group of religious men not including Jews, Samaritans, or heathens, and he found such a group in the disciples of John, '. . . so it becomes more likely that this scene is not at all a historic event . . .'.[3] Meyer's suggestion is 'ingenious', but there appears to be no external or internal evidence to confirm his conclusions. What might come out of it for our purpose, however, is that even in Meyer's suggestion the atmosphere of the Spirit or a local Pentecost was deemed necessary to give the touch of authority to Paul.

Corinth, of course, would be one of the places encouraged to expect those Pentecostal happenings. Indeed, something did happen. It did not make much difference to the spirit of fellowship within the Church. The Church at Corinth was still divided in a distressing manner, with unfortunate quarrels in many places. Nevertheless, the folk could speak with tongues in an amazing way, and that seemed most important!

Glossolalia was so much in evidence and so much prized at Corinth that most scholars have suggested that it was the result of local pagan and heathen influence. It is suggested that glossolalia at Corinth was of Gentile origin, since most of the converts to Christianity would be Gentile. That something similar to glossolalia was not unknown in the Gentile world is indeed certain. H. D. Wendland makes the usual suggestion that when Paul refers to the Corinthians being 'carried away'

[3] E. Meyer, *Ursprung und Anfänge des Christentums*, III.114.

(1 Corinthians 12¹) it is something characteristic of the heathen religion to which the Corinthians were clinging before they adopted Christianity. He suggests, further, that the glossolalia at Corinth was a dangerous form of syncretism. It was a holding to something which was part of a pagan custom, that which was fascinating and exciting, hence came the attempt to legalize it by fitting it into the Christian tradition at Corinth.[4]

Reports of Irenæus about the gnostic magician Marcus and his prophetess prove that in the second century similar utterances of unintelligible ecstatic speeches were known.[5] These utterances may be connected with Hellenistic prophecy.[6] Some scholars are of the opinion that the 'voces mysticæ', the mysterious meaningless words and sounds of the ancient magic papyri, are connected with the stammering ecstatic speeches, probably the 'language of ghosts' developed in the old-time religion of Corinth.[7] Or again, it is suggested that the notions 'enter into God' and 'to receive God or the Spirit' alternate in heathen literature in the same way as Paul uses the ideas 'to be in Christ' and 'bear the image of Christ'. The poet thus possessed, after comparing himself with the seer or prophet, likes to describe the entering of the particular god—such an entrance often resulting in the ecstasy which produced glossolalia. Lucian, using an old Hellenistic report, describes the ecstasy of Pythia. The god enters the woman. He expels her ψυχή, being the individuality, from her breast. It is he alone who lives in her, and now she recognizes and knows all events from the beginning. Freed from the bonds of space and time she bursts forth into ecstatic and uncontrolled speech.[8] So it is suggested that here again is a clue to the background which brought the phenomenon of glossolalia to Corinth.

Some suggest that the cult of Bacchus offers a clue to the ecstatic of the Corinthian Church. The Bacchic celebrations and trances were 'helped' by intoxication by wine; wild dancing followed with shouts and ecstatic stammering of sounds and words (*Mysteries of Bacchus*, Livy 13.13).[9] 'Theologus,' referring to this Bacchic dancing, compares it with 1 Corinthians 13¹, 'sounding brass and tinkling cymbal', saying that this phrase forced itself upon Paul's mind because he knew

---

[4] *Das Neue Testament Deutsche*, II.347.
[5] H. Lietzmann, *Handbuch zum Neuen Testament*, I.70f.
[6] R. Reitzenstein, *Die hellenistischen Mysterienreligionen*, pp. 219ff.
[7] H. D. Wendland, op. cit., p. 364.   [8] R. Reitzenstein, op. cit., p. 45.
[9] ibid., p. 96; also Philo, *De Vita cont.*, 473M.

that the Corinthian cults were accustomed to using such instruments to produce the ecstasy which accompanied glossolalia.[10] Theophilus (II.xxviii.136) reports a heathen word about speaking with tongues, namely the famous 'εὐοῖ'. The word repeated over and over was used to induce an ecstatic state. We know of such a word from the 'wars of the Cévennes'. It was uttered by the Camisards whenever they encountered the royal armies. Brueys in his history writes: *'Les prophêts et les prophétesses s'avançèrent au devant des troupes* [of the Camisards] *avec un air furieux en soufflant sur elles de toute la force et criant à haute voix: "Tartar, Tartara".*'[11]

Celsus gives a report of certain false prophets who, for the sake of impressing with strange speech, used words from barbaric languages and then used a stranger series of sounds for fraudulent 'speaking with tongues'. According to the teaching of the Gnostics, souls yearning for the union with the 'father of light' invoked the 'ghosts of the air' by means of these mysterious magic words and stammered phrases. Schmidt says that often this glossolalia was a senseless linking together of vowels, e.g. ιεουα, ιεα, ωιεου, ιεου, then there would be real words inserted. Another form was senseless connexions of vowels and consonants:

ζωζηζαζ, ζαωζωζ, χωζως, ζωζηζα, χωζωζαζζα.
ζαζηζω, αζωζα, ζωζαωχα, χωζωαζαω, ζωζηαζα . . . .

Everyone repeats these words on and on like clockwork. They are, of course, unreal, like the papyri of the magicians.[12] Clement of Alexandria, referring to Plato, writes that Plato deduced from the observation of cases of possession certain theories as to the language of the gods which seems to be spoken by the mouths of the possessed. Plato attributes a dialect also to the gods, forming this conjecture especially from demoniacs who do not speak their own language but that of the demons who have possessed them.[13]

Another instance of glossolalia in the pagan world is that of

[10] 'Theologus', *Prussian Annual Reports*, LXXXVII.223f.
[11] Brueys, *Histoire du fanaticism de notre temps*, I, Sec.182, cited by Weinel, op. cit., p. 73.
[12] Schmidt, *Gnostiche Schriften in coptischen Sprache*, VIII.xii.146ff. See also Weinel, *Die Wirkungen des Geistes*, pp. 72–101. Cited by Lietzmann, *Handbuch zum Neuen Testament*, pp. 68ff. Lists of such magical voices are to be found in *Pap. Lond.*, I.255ff., and in Cabrol *Dictionnaire d'archéologie chrétienne*, I.137ff.; cf. *Pap. Lond.*, I, No. 121, pp. 102 and 561ff.
[13] Oesterreich, *Possession*, p. 159.

the Delphian prophetess, whose cries were 'interpreted' by attendant priests in a manner that reminds one of the Christian meetings reported to be taking place at Corinth. Celsus, as quoted by Origen, tells of pagan fanatics 'who utter unintelligible, crazy and jumbled words, the sense of which no one can make out and which everybody interprets according to his pleasure . . .'. Many unknown men assume the movements of fortune-tellers within the sanctuaries and outside. They roam about like beggars. They visit towns and barracks . . . they write detailed threats, then add unintelligible, half-mad and obscure words, which nobody can explain because there is nothing to explain; but every madman, every impostor may turn such speech to his own advantage. Celsus says that these so-called prophets admitted afterwards their cheating and their invention of such unintelligible words![14]

It is quite evident that in numerous cults of the time some kind of glossolalia was probably practised. Many conclude that it was for this reason that the practice found its way so readily and easily into a community like that of Corinth, which had been formed from a pagan population. So P. Volz is typical of the majority of scholars when they give their judgement upon the question of Corinthian glossolalia. 'A vigorous infiltration of ideas and customs from pagan Asia Minor is obvious. Christendom expanded in Asia Minor rapidly and powerfully, whilst in Palestine the religion of Jesus only slowly advanced. Asia Minor was previously moved by deep religious excitements. Many different nations passed through this country and many new religions were preached here. Now Christianity made its appearance. It was at once hailed as a miraculous and spiritualistic movement. The new believers were in a state of happiest excitement, and because of this the influence of the mysteries of Asia Minor were potential. . . .'[15] That is the usual treatment of glossolalia at Corinth, that it was a symptom of the exuberant religious enthusiasm of Paul's Corinthian converts with its psychological roots in the mobile excitable Greek temperament.[16]

Is there another place where we can seek the origins of Corinthian glossolalia? Prof. T. W. Manson suggests: 'The most

---

[14] *Origen. c. Celsum*, vii. 9.   [15] *Der Geist Gottes*, p. 197.
[16] T. W. Manson, *St Paul in Ephesus* (3); Reprint from *Bulletin of John Rylands Library*, XXVI, No. 1 (Oct.-Nov. 1941), p. 16.

natural place to seek for the origin of glossolalia is not Corinth, but Jerusalem.'[17] We feel that this is the best explanation. The theory that it was borrowed from paganism is quite unwarranted. We need to remind ourselves again that the inheritance of the primitive Church is Jewish—both in the religious ideas of the new faith and the psychological dispositions which moulded it. The religious environment of the disciples and of the earliest converts is significant when discussing this problem of the Corinthian Church.

We have already referred to the revival of the prophetic consciousness which opens the era of the New Testament. The prophet and the ecstatic experience of the prophet had lost their earlier authenticity, but a faint hope remained that the prophets would rise again. Hundreds of the common folk looked for the advent of a new prophetic era. We saw how this expectancy was behind the birth of Jesus. Then came John the Baptist; the stage was set for '*the* Prophet' and Jesus came. There followed a triumphant ministry in the power of the same Spirit which possessed the prophets of old. Death came, but the darkness of the shadow of death was penetrated through and through with light, for Jesus rose from the dead. There followed the empowering experience of the Spirit. Ordinary men and women were possessed of the same power that controlled Gideon, the same power that gave the prophet his authority. The Christian faith was a rebirth of the old prophetic consciousness now centred around the person of Jesus in a new overpowering love relationship. In future, wherever the Christian preachers went they would declare that the glories of the past had come again, and in the experience of the Spirit with all its physical accompaniments there was something rooted in the old experience of prophetic consciousness. Here then was the origin of glossolalia in the Christian Church.

In every pagan rite or cult we have mentioned above, the ecstatic experience was *sought*, and in many cases artificial means were used to induce a state of uncontrollable excitement which became false ecstasy. But in the New Testament there is no artificiality; ecstasy comes first, and the strange utterances are the outward sign of the inward condition. The Spirit comes upon the persons and then they speak with tongues.

We have already referred to the influence of the group in the

[17] T. W. Manson, *St Paul in Ephesus* (3); Reprint from *Bulletin of John Rylands Library*, XXVI, No. 1 (Oct.-Nov. 1941), p. 17.

Early Church. The experience which came to the believers on the day of Pentecost became, we suggest, a 'norm' or 'test' experience for the whole Church. The tendency was to make a rigid rule about the faith; differences in personality were forgotten—a local Pentecost must be expected by every group. The Spirit would surely fall, and when the Spirit did fall their reception of the gift would be manifest by certain marked phenomena, i.e. the strange utterances of glossolalia. That seems to have become almost a rule. It was when such expectancy became dangerous and when the leaders of a group became pedantic about this thing that Paul felt constrained to attempt to make the issue clear.

The same tendency to make rigid rules about religious experience is an age-long danger. In certain evangelical groups the 'sudden conversion' became a type of all conversions. Indeed this was almost declared to be the only real conversion, and a quiet surrender of the life to God in a less dramatic fashion was regarded with suspicion. Visitors from an 'Elim' community were heard to remark about two hard-working and devout Christian workers: 'It is a pity that Sister G. and Mr B. have so much, and yet haven't the Spirit.' When asked to elucidate the latter statement, the Elim visitors declared they knew the workers had not 'the Spirit' because 'they never spoke with tongues'. There was the danger of making a rule about religious experience. The primitive Church, however, was so overcome by the new power in its midst that all the precision of logic was shattered. Pentecost had meant life, vision, power, and expansion of the Kingdom: it was a revival of all that was glorious and triumphant in Hebrew faith and Palestinian piety. So it became the great expectation of every new group to have another Pentecost. From time to time we are given a report of these outbursts; they are mentioned in Acts—already referred to—and took place in the Palestinian Church. In contrast to being influenced by pagan cult and custom the phenomena described by Paul in 1 Corinthians seem akin to these Palestinian outbursts; at Ephesus, Thessalonica, Colossæ, we have discovered evidence of the same sort of thing.

We suggest then that glossolalia made its way to Corinth in that manner. It was part of Apostolic teaching to encourage a 'local Pentecost'. The preachers were shocked that this had not been experienced at Ephesus in the early days, and they set about putting that matter right.

Most of the commentaries take it for granted that glossolalia was something which had been at Corinth for a long time, that it was something of old standing, belonging to a pagan past, which the new converts at Corinth tacked on to the new faith. Paul, however, when he is dealing with the problem, does not deal with the problem as an old one. He would have been the first to deal vigorously with any kind of dangerous syncretism, seeing that for him 'old things are passed away', the 'light' has no 'fellowship' with darkness. He makes it quite clear in many places that the Christian is not subject to ordinances. Had the Corinthians been in danger of such syncretism Paul would have lifted his voice in protest, for he was eighteen months at Corinth and saw the early growth of the Church. Paul, however, does not treat the topic in this fashion, nor does he speak of the problems as those that are quite familiar to the Corinthian Church. He deals elaborately with it as though it is a new thing about which the Corinthians needed detailed instructions and guidance.[18] They had misunderstood earlier teaching and were misusing something which was intended to be a power in the Christian community. Moreover, it does not appear that Paul had included any teaching regarding the phenomenon in his preaching. There is no doubt that had it been part of his normal procedure he would, during the eighteen months of his ministry, have given directions about its place in the Christian programme. Dr Manson writes: 'If his [Paul's] exposition of the Gospel had included this phenomenon at all, doubtless he would have given some kind of instruction about its place in the scheme of Christian values and the importance to be attached to it in comparison with other aspects of the Christian life. The fact that at this late date he has to begin an explanation is evidence that the thing is something of a novelty in the Corinthian Church. And the fact that Paul can thank God that he has done more of it himself than the entire Corinthian community, strongly suggests that the practice has not yet reached any very imposing proportions there, especially in view of the fact that Paul himself does not appear to have gone out of his way to seek experiences of this sort. . . .'[19]

What had happened? We have been suggesting that a catechetical question was, 'Did ye receive the Holy Ghost?', and that every effort would be made to experience a 'local Pentecost'. Yet here Paul is working against certain happen-

---

[18] Manson, op. cit., p. 17. [19] ibid., p. 18.

ings. At Ephesus he encourages the little group on to this vital Spirit experience, whilst here at Corinth he hints that the whole thing is beset with dangers—dangers within the fellowship and outside. It appears that Paul has seen a danger signal.

We must go farther and ask from whence came the danger which Paul saw, and what constituted the danger thus seen. The danger most probably came from the Cephas party which had made such a mark on the Corinthian community. Cephas himself might have visited the district, but in any case, certain of the Petrine groups were doing enthusiastic work. Wherever the influence of this party moved, Paul sensed danger. At almost every council he and the Cephas party clashed. This clash has nothing to do with primacy in the apostleship—in any case, by A.D. 48 or 49 James was probably number one. It was a clash over principles and tendencies. The Cephas party was narrow. They took the nature of the Hebrew-Jewish roots of the new faith too rigidly. The new faith was a revival—with new additions and allegiances—of something that had been in the consciousness of the nation before. Those things belonging to the 'old-time religion' the Cephas party said they must keep. Circumcision was a rite of the Old Order; the Judaizers, and amongst these the Cephas party was chief, demanded that the rite of circumcision must be kept in the New Faith. So, too, the Law was just as necessary to the new as the old.

Now it was with these conservative prejudices that Paul clashed. He was a Hebrew of the Hebrews, and of the highest tradition amongst the Hebrews, but the new faith was a fulfilment of the old, and certain cherished prejudices had to go. This old spectre of the clash between the old and new appeared again at Corinth. We might say that both Paul and the Cephas party encouraged believers to expect the Pentecostal experience of the Spirit, but what they meant by such teaching was different. The Cephas party was concerned with accidentals. They knew how the old prophets threw themselves about in ecstatic frenzy; they knew what had happened at Pentecost. Not only did they know this, but they demanded that wherever the local Church developed they must show signs of being in the real tradition by giving evidence of similar physical and psychical accompaniments. So when the new believers were taught to expect a local Pentecost, it must be of a special type and special order.

It seems that there was a danger of a ritual developing even about receiving the Spirit. This was the danger against which Paul fought at Corinth. It was not such a danger elsewhere, because we have no records of a Cephas party forming itself so strongly anywhere else. This is significant. It would appear that wherever the Cephas party was, there was this danger. Paul saw that the community at Corinth was being compelled to produce a certain specific brand of Spirit-possession that was accompanied by a glossolalia which conformed to prescribed type. Paul believed in the 'local Pentecost', but he never gave rules about it. He cared little for physical accompaniments, but he was deeply concerned about inward holiness that made men moral giants. Hence came his directions and timely warning to the Corinthian Church. He was working against artificiality; fighting against the demand which we suggest came from the Cephas party to produce this particular fruit of the Spirit. Just as he fought all attempts to bring the rites or legalism of Judaism into the New Faith, so he fought the tendency to make Christian witness and experience a stereotyped thing. The Cephas party was trying to make Corinthian believers act and respond in a uniform way; Paul pitted himself against this tendency.

It may be that we have no record of his giving earlier instruction about the Spirit because from the early days he sensed the danger that the Cephas party had brought, and in the earlier days the primacy of Peter meant a good deal. So Dr Manson confirms this point of view as he concludes his discussion of this problem. 'I venture, therefore, to think that what the Apostle is dealing with in these chapters is not a surfeit of glossolalia at Corinth, but a demand which was being made on the Church to produce this particular fruit of the Spirit. I suggest that the demand came from the leaders of the Cephas party and was part of the concerted move to instil Palestinian piety and Palestinian orthodoxy into the Corinthian Church. Paul's converts were being told that here was something most important, indeed absolutely essential to the Christian life.'[20] Paul makes it quite clear what he thinks about the importance of glossolalia and how many things take precedence of it in the Christian life.[21]

---

[20] Manson, op. cit., p. 18.
[21] cf. F. C. Synge, 'The Holy Spirit in the Gospels and Acts', *Church Quarterly Review*, July 1935, p. 211.

It is fitting to end this discussion by considering what, for Paul, was the true nature and significance of the glossolalia at Corinth. This is determined in the light of Chapters 12–14. One might say that the dissension illustrates more clearly than anything else in his writings the Apostle's wonderful sanity of judgement. We have to remember that so often glossolalia became far more than an accidental physical accompaniment of an uprush of spiritual emotion. It seems to have become an accepted part of Church activity. There is little doubt that to the whole Church of the time glossolalia was an impressive fact in Christian worship. Some accepted it as cardinal proof of the divine origin of the Gospel. To excel in this extraordinary gift, which marked the man directly favoured by the Spirit, was the chief ambition of every believer. Paul does not doubt that it is a supernatural gift, and declares that he knows more about it than many in Corinth, from his own personal experience. He advises his converts to exercise it sparingly, and to set their hearts on other gifts, more useful though less spectacular. Above all, he perceives that this gift, for all its excitement and seeming flavour of the old prophetic consciousness, is not to be compared with the supreme gifts of faith, hope, and love.[22]

The chief fact on which Paul lays stress in his account of tongues is that they are unintelligible. Dr E. F. Scott[22] says that it is from this point of view that Paul assesses their value. To hear them is like listening to an unknown language or to musical sounds which convey no tune. Paul does not say that for this reason the tongues are worthless, for the man who utters them might receive a personal benefit. But this benefit is not shared by those who listen to him. The believers really constitute one body, the members were meant to serve one another, and the good of each must in some way contribute to the good of all. If this is the test then glossolalia is found wanting. The Spirit is bestowed upon the Church for the advancement of the Church at large, and not for the emotional enjoyment of the individual. 'When the individual *alone* is helped by its gift, it misses its true object. The very nature of the Spirit demands that whatever it bestows on one should be communicated through him to all.'

Paul concludes that the tongues are lower than certain other gifts, but he admits that in three directions they have a real value. Dr Scott[23] puts these points as follows:

[22] Scott, E. F., *The Spirit in the New Testament*, p. 102.   [23] ibid., pp. 103–6.

(1) The man who speaks in a tongue is himself edified, for God understands the words which for men have no meaning. The 'tongue' is a spiritual language for speaking 'mysteries', that is to say, it gives expression to thoughts and aspirations which can utter themselves in this way and no other. The inarticulate sounds have all the value of intelligible prayer. Paul says in the very chapter in which he criticizes tongues that he himself was in the habit of using them in his private devotions, although he refrained from using them in the assembly (1 Corinthians 12[18f.]). He found that they afforded him a real outlet to pent-up feelings which he could not express in words. This is the suggested meaning of the familiar passage in Romans (8[26]): 'And in like manner the Spirit also helpeth our infirmity: for we know not how to pray as we ought; but the Spirit himself maketh intercession for us with inarticulate groanings. . . .' Here was a man who made more effort than any other to think out the meaning of the Gospel, yet he could not define in words what he felt to be deepest in his religion. He fell back on that confused utterance of the Spirit, believing that God would understand.

(2) Again, Scott observes, Paul holds that though the tongues were unintelligible, they were not without value, even for the common worshipper. There were some in the assembly who could apprehend what was conveyed in them. In any case there were those who possessed the specific gift of 'interpretation' and could explain in ordinary language what the speaker meant. One might surmise that in most cases the 'tongues' did not signify anything very mysterious. The speaker might suggest by the tone of his voice or by the special 'kind of tongue' he employed, the contrition or thanksgiving or longing to which he strove to give utterance. It is probable that there would be those present who by a natural tact and sympathy trained by practice in this particular duty, would be able to discern at least the general drift of spiritual language.

(3) Dr Scott's final point is that apart from the meaning to the worshipper himself, and to his fellow-worshippers, the tongues had a value for the outside world. Paul reminds the Corinthians that the sight of a 'congregation engaged in this strange practice was apt to excite the mockery of unbelievers, who saw in it nothing but madness. None the less, it was a "sign" to them, a proof that a divine power was at work in the Church' (1 Corinthians 14[23]). Is Paul suggesting that even for the un-

believer witnessing 'tongues' it could be the dawning of new light—people might come to mock and remain to pray?

It seems probable that only glossolalia and kindred phenomena were at first attributed to the Spirit. Paul battled against this notion and fought on until it was realized that the activity of the Spirit could not be limited to one peculiar phase in the life of the Fellowship. He encouraged the belief that since the Spirit had been given by Christ for the advancement of His cause, it must be operative in all that belonged to Christian worship and enterprise. The Church was distinguished from all other societies in that it was governed by the Spirit.

It must be of fundamental importance to understand this fact. 'There has been continual and endless controversy as to the constitution of the primitive Church. Every later sect has had a natural desire to see in itself the true representative of the Apostolic model. It has been assumed that the original Church was similar in character to that which grew out of it and was an organized body with an official ministry.' The truth seems, however, that the disciples rejected the very idea of a human-dictated organization and especially did Paul attack this idea, though Paul was ready to give regulations if there was any danger of a menace to the fundamentals of the Faith. As we have seen, when one party attempted to organize a common experience, he would not have personality violated in any such way. There was a genuine attempt to let the Spirit guide and control. 'The Spirit had come in the place of Jesus. He Himself had once presided over His company of disciples, but now that He was gone, the Spirit directed them in His stead, and in the manner that He desired. Everything like organization was, at first, avoided as contrary to the inner-nature of the Church. It was the community of the Spirit, and must be willing in all things to order itself by that divine guidance.'[24]

This was the conviction that in the early days led to a sort of communism. As the Church grew in numbers the strict equality became impracticable. The ideal was one that could not be realized and effort to press it too literally would have thrown its whole life into hopeless confusion. Even in the first days, several of the disciples seem to have taken upon themselves an informal ministry and little by little the Church evolved a strict organization. By the end of the first century its leaders had become officials, with their spheres of duty rigidly pre-

[24] Scott, E. F., *The Spirit in the New Testament*, p. 108f.

scribed, and it would appear that the belief that they were organs of the Spirit had hardened into a mechanical theory—this became a new problem. At the outset, the idea of spiritual control was taken seriously; subsequently 'acts of the Spirit' seem to disappear, thwarted by organization and ecclesiastical regulation. It was against this tendency to organize at the expense of the direction of the Spirit that the Montanists fought. The Montanists, with all their fanaticism and fantastic prejudices, are symbols of that element which always warns against the dangers which beset life. The Spirit is barricaded out of life by human schemes and plans, so it is fitting that we should end our discussion of the gift of the Spirit with a brief survey of Montanism.

CHAPTER TEN

Montanism: A Revival of Prophecy

WE HAVE seen that the primitive Church in its first stage was a mystical fellowship, i.e. a fellowship bound together not by external organization, but by the power of the experience of the Divine Presence among the members. At this time the Holy Spirit was thought of as a power coming from *without, into* the person. The Divine incoming was conceived as an invasion. The atmosphere of this invasion was charged with wonder and the early apostles speak of 'speaking with tongues' as though it were a regular gift to be looked for wherever the Spirit came upon men. Moreover, wherever Christianity went in the apostolic period there seems to have been a manifestation of the spirit of prophecy. It was not confined to men, though women prophets were not encouraged. There was a height of enthusiasm, a quality of faith which undoubtedly carried persons beyond their normal powers. This resulted in an uninterrupted succession of prophecy and this prophetic ministry was one of the great creative agencies in the formation and development of the Early Church.[1]

We have mentioned that women prophesied in the Corinthian Church where prophetic powers were to some extent a matter of reputation (1 Corinthians 11^5). At Rome it was a recognized gift (Romans 12^6). At Antioch a famine in Claudius' reign had been foretold by Agabus, who came with other prophets from Jerusalem, and among the names of prophets resident there in the normal state of the Christian Church we have those of Symeon Niger, Lucius of Cyrene, Mnason, besides Barnabas and Saul, who ministered to the Lord in public worship, and received instruction from the Holy Spirit (Acts 11^{27}, 13^1). Judas and Silas were two who exercised their prophetic gift at Antioch and elsewhere. At Cæsarea four daughters of Philip the Evangelist were prophesying, and later they were joined by Agabus. He used the old prophetic symbolism, bind-

---

[1] See Note C, p. 126 below, for note on Paul's discrimination between 'predictive' prophecy and prophecy as 'preaching'.

ing Paul's hands and feet and saying: 'Thus saith the Holy Spirit. . . .'[2]

While prophecy was at its height there was no fixed and rigid organization in the Church. It was held together by inspired personalities. Both Acts and the Pauline epistles imply guidance by responsible leaders, especially apostles and elders, but these leaders are chosen 'by the Holy Spirit'. The Corinthian circle showed a liberty that was dangerous, but Paul had declared as a permanent principle: 'Where the Spirit of the Lord is, there is liberty.' The one principle which Paul lays down as far as *restraint* is concerned is that the gift shall edify. The Early Church was influenced more by suggestion than command and rigid rule; everything was 'under the Spirit', even the itinerant ministry which was growing up.

The order of prophets we have observed had been well established and generally recognized in the Church of the first century. Paul ranks them after the apostles (1 Corinthians 12^{28}; cf. Ephesians 4^{11}). 'Quench not the Spirit, despise not prophesying' (1 Thessalonians 5$^{19-20}$). The Church had been 'built on the foundation of the apostles and prophets' (Ephesians 2^{20}), and the mystery of Christ had been 'revealed unto his Holy apostles and prophets in the Spirit' (2^{5}). In the Apocalypse, 'prophets and saints' are the two most distinctive classes of believers (Revelation 10^{7}, 11^{18}, 16^{16}, 18$^{20f.,24}$).

The order survived into the second century, although it was being gradually superseded by the episcopate. Justin Martyr claims that 'the prophetic gift remains with us even today',[3] and 'one receives the Spirit of understanding, another of counsel, another of strength, another of healing, another of foreknowledge, another of tending, another of the fear of God'.[4] These gifts had been distributed by one or two to the Hebrew prophets, but they all found rest in Christ, and He 'imparts them to those who believe in Him'.[5] Irenæus also appears to refer to prophecy and other gifts of the Spirit as contemporary facts, and he limits their operation within the (Catholic) Church.[6] By Origen's time, however, 'these signs had diminished, although there were still traces of the Holy Spirit's presence in a few who had their souls purified by the gospel'.[7]

We are in another world. The period of free, spontaneous,

---

[2] Acts 15^{32}, 21^{10}. (N.B. εἶπεν may imply the ancient form כה אמר יהוה.)
[3] *Dialog.*, 82.   [4] ibid., 39.   [5] ibid., 87.
[6] *Adv. Haer.*, II.xxxii.4, V.vi.1.   [7] *C. Celsum*, vii. 8, 11.

MONTANISM: A REVIVAL OF PROPHECY

uprushing, spiritual life has passed away. The prophet has well-nigh disappeared. The prophet speaking by revelation has yielded to the Bishop ruling with authority. The prophetic ministry grew weak and poor. People began to be suspicious that the claim of divine guidance was a cloak under which prophets voiced their own desires, etc.[8] The conquering power of the Spirit seemed to be dying out. How would the Church be kept pure? A clergy with authority seemed the only way.

Dissatisfied with the worldliness and rigid organization of the Church in the year A.D. 157, Montanus, a 'converted' priest[9] of Phrygia commenced a crusade (not far from the region of Paul's Galatian Churches). He preached against the prevailing licentiousness, and called for a return to the vigorous faith and simple spirit-devoted life of the early days of Christianity. His zeal and evident sincerity evoked much response, particularly among women, and Montanus seems to have been always attended on his journeys by two devoted 'Prophetesses', named Maximilla and Prisca or Priscilla. Success seems to have caused Montanus to lose his balance. He even claimed to be the Incarnation of the Paraclete, and declared that his utterances and decisions should be received as divinely inspired revelations of God's will. He called on his followers to break entirely with the world, to give up marriage and earthly ties, to live in a state of frequent ecstasy and vision, to expect martyrdom. He preached severest asceticism and most austere continence: he claimed the supremacy of the individual conscience acting under direct inspiration of the Holy Spirit and denied the rights of the community or Church to order men's lives. The only control he would recognize was 'spirit-control'.

The new prophets were first received with enthusiasm, for 'there was a sibylline strain in these simple, rural people which made them ready for religious fervour and ecstatic visions'. But the authorities were dangerously hostile. Consequently, the bishops of Asia Minor condemned Montanus and his teaching and

[8] cf. Decline of Prophecy in Judaism. When the prophet prophesied 'good' if it was convenient to his income, the lying prophet appeared. The discovery that selfish motives were dominating the prophetic cult soon led to their abandonment as the voices of authority. Cf. also the *Didache*. The warning against false prophets and the admonition, 'Appoint for yourselves, therefore, bishops and deacons . . . despise them not: for they are your honourable men along with prophets and teachers'—*Doctrina Apost.*, 7–15.

[9] Those who denounce his prophecies say that Montanus was formerly a pagan priest, possibly a priest of Cybele.

excommunicated him and his followers. Forbidden to reform the Church from within, Montanus seceded and claimed orthodoxy for himself alone. He called his followers Pneumatics (πνευματικοί), those led by the Spirit, as opposed to Psychici (ψυχικοί), the natural, who were in his judgement of a lower order. The schism soon began to attract attention outside the limits of Phrygia, and famous Bishops, Dionysius of Corinth, Apollinarius of Hierapolis, Serapion of Antioch, were drawn into the fray.[10] By A.D. 173 the controversy had reached Rome, and in 177 the confessors of Lyons obtained from Pope Eleutherus a condemnation of Montanism. It was on the point of being set aside by his successor, Victor, when Praxeas arrived from Asia, and the condemnation was confirmed:[11] apostles of Montanism, such as Proclus, attempted to reverse this decision, but in vain: Rome refused to give countenance to the 'Spirituals'.

However, the appeal for stricter personal discipline and asceticism and the claim for more direct personal spirit revelation had attracted the ardent soul of Tertullian at Carthage. It may be that he had come into contact with the Montanists while still at Rome. Evidently it was not quantity but quality that Tertullian looked for. In *De jejunio adv. Pysch.* xi he speaks of the force of his 'inexperienced' few being greater than even the multitude of orthodox: 'But all this I suppose is unknown to those who are disturbed at our teaching, or has been discovered by mere reading perhaps (of the Holy Scripture) without the addition of the inner meaning, according to the greater forcefulness of our inexperienced as compared with your most glorious crowd of Psychici. . . .' In another passage he says: 'Your

[10] Eusebius, *Hist. Eccl.*, V.xvi.10, etc.

[11] Tertullian is strong in his condemnation of Praxeas: the following quotation is not out of place here: 'For Praxeas it was who first imported from Asia to Rome this kind of perversity—a man in other ways unquiet—puffed up with pride of confessorship merely on the strength of a short annoyance of imprisonment without further hardship; whereas even though he had given his body to be burned, he would have gained nothing by it, not having the Love of God, whose gifts too he has fought against. He it was who when the then Bishop of Rome was ready to recognize the prophecies of Montanus, Prisca, and Maximilla, and in consequence of that recognition to give his peace to the Churches of Asia and Phrygia—he by making false statements about the prophets themselves and their Churches, and by urging the authority of the Bishop's predecessors, obliged him to recall the letters of peace he had already sent out, and to give up his purpose of acknowledging the gift. Thus Praxeas managed two of the devil's businesses in Rome: he drove out prophecy and brought in heresy; he put to flight the Comforter and crucified the Father.' (*Adv. Prax.*, I.) H. M. Gwatkin, *Selections from Early Christian Writers*, pp. 127ff.

Church may consist only of three persons. It is better sometimes to avoid seeing your crowds of brethren. . . . Many are called, few chosen. Christ does not seek the man who is ready to follow the broad path, but the narrow; and therefore the Paraclete is necessary, who guides into all the truth, who gives patience in all adversity.'[12] So 'where three are present, there is the Church, even in the absence of an ordained minister'.[13]

It would appear that these devotees were not necessarily excluded from Church membership. On the contrary, we find a Montanist sister habitually seeing visions during divine service in church, which are regularly reported and examined afterwards.[14] The same fact—the presence of Montanist wardens in church—is implied in *De virg. vel.* xvii, in which passage mention is made of the vision of an angel to a sister, prescribing the length of the veil to be worn during the Psalms or any commemoration of God. Moreover, the open break with the orthodox Church on the part of Tertullian came after A.D. 212. It was not long before Tertullian broke away from the old Montanist body and founded a separate order of Tertullianists which lasted two hundred years.

Montanism, then, was the one great uprising during the first three centuries against the officialism and ecclesiasticism which was slowly taking the place of the immediate working of the Holy Spirit, and which was banishing the prophet from the Church. Moreover, the disappearance and suppression of prophecy is well illustrated in the Church's attitude toward Montanism.[15]

The imperial system became the type of Church government, and with that the entire nature of Christianity was in danger of undergoing a complete change. The fellowship of believers became a rigid ecclesiastical organization. Faith which had been inward trust and immediate response to a living Christ became 'the faith'—a fixed and often lifeless dogma of orthodoxy. The simple remembrances became magical celebrations. The free and spontaneous exercise of spiritual gifts gave place to an inflexible system of form and ritual. These were momentous changes, and it was natural that there should be protest and reaction. The literary remains of the second century are meagre, but there are indications that in some districts a Christianity like that of the early days persisted.

[12] *De fuga in pers.*, xiv.
[13] *De exh. cast.*, vii: *Ubi tres, ecclesia est, licet laici.*
[14] *De anima*, lx.
[15] Rufus M. Jones, *Studies in Mystical Religion*, p. 35.

Montanism did not introduce new doctrines; it was not a new conception of God, nor of the world, nor of salvation. It was an attempt to realize in the Church the promise of Christ that the Paraclete should come to lead men into all truth and to enable them to do greater things than he did. In the spirit of the Hebrew prophets they raised a passion for purity and holiness in the people of God, and with this they expected an annihilation of the wicked pagan world by the arrival of the New Jerusalem from heaven.

De Soyres[16] when dealing with the tenets of Montanism gives a six-fold list:

(*a*) Doctrine of the Trinity,
(*b*) The Work of the Spirit,
(*c*) The Theory of the Church,
(*d*) The Sacraments,
(*e*) Discipline,
(*f*) Eschatology.

For our purpose we shall confine ourselves to the second tenet, the work of the Spirit in relation especially to prophecy. This seems to be the most striking feature of Montanism—its revival of prophecy, the attempt to put the authority of the Christian Church in a succession of divinely inspired preacher prophets. Church leaders were busy constructing an authoritative system. Montanism tried to cry aloud: 'All is of God . . . except the Lord build the house, they labour in vain. . . .' Its prophets taught essentially the priesthood of all believers. They insisted that ministers were made by God alone, and they undertook to form a Church of saints.

Montanus and his followers claimed to have received a direct revelation of God, as did the whole succession of prophets. Hippolytus says of them: 'They have been deceived by two females, Priscilla and Maximilla by name, whom they hold to be prophetesses, asserting that into them the Paraclete spirit entered. . . . They implicitly believe what they utter. They magnify these females above the Apostles and every gift of Grace, so that some of them go so far as to say that there is in them something more than Christ. These people agree with the Church in acknowledging the Father of the universe to be God . . . they also acknowledge all that the Gospel testifies of Christ. But they introduce novelties, fasts and feasts and meals

---

[16] *Montanism and the Primitive Church*, ad loc.

of radishes, giving these females as their authority. . . .'[17] Philaster wrote: 'They hold that the full gift of the Holy Spirit was not granted by Christ to his apostles, but to their false prophets.' Augustine states: 'They declare that the promised advent of the Holy Spirit took place in themselves.' These were writing as the enemies of Montanism.

Tertullian, who, as we have seen, in later life became a Montanist, never loses an opportunity of asserting the superior insight employed by those who hearkened to the Paraclete through the mouths of the prophets or prophetesses, nor does he deal gently with those who made Montanism a heresy.[18]

There is a report in the writings of Eusebius which says: 'Montanus, a recently baptized Christian, had allowed "the fiend" to enter into him because he was excited by excessive ambition. So he was filled by a spirit and in a mad ecstasy he enthusiastically and suddenly spattered out odd words. . . . Some of them that heard his bastard utterances rebuked him as one possessed of a devil . . . remembering the Lord's warning to guard against the coming of false prophets. . . . But others were carried away and not a little elated, thinking themselves possessed of the Holy Spirit and of the gift of prophecy. And he also stirred up two women and filled them with the bastard spirit so that they uttered demented, absurd, and irresponsible sayings. . . . And these people blasphemed the whole Catholic Church under heaven, under the influence of their presumptuous spirit, because the Church granted to the spirit of false prophecy neither honour nor admission.'[19] It appears that here is a reference to glossolalia among the Montanists; the 'demented, absurd, and irresponsible speech' which was reported was most certainly 'tongue-speech'. An overpowering ecstasy is mentioned which to the amazed onlooker demonstrates that the prophet is possessed by a spirit compelling him to speak. Whatever the Spirit commands must be done.[20] There is the pulse and push of authority within. So, too, the prophetesses suddenly begin to speak; they are overpowered and speak in sudden ecstasy, surprising all the onlookers.

[17] *Ref. Omn. Haer.*, viii. 19. Cited by H. Bettenson, *Documents of the Christian Church*, p. 109.
[18] See note [11] *supra*.
[19] *Hist. Eccl.*, xvi.7f.
[20] cf. the Old Testament prophet who could do nothing else but prophesy and whose conviction was 'Thus saith the Lord . . .', or Paul, who declared, 'Woe is me if I preach not the Gospel'.

Montanus describes his own experience—or rather it is the 'Lord' who speaks:

> Lo, man is like a lyre,
> And I fly nearer like a plectrum,
> Man sleeps,
> O watch,
> Lo, it is the Lord!
> Taking from their breasts the hearts of men
> And giving a new heart to men . . . .

Man thinks he is sleeping and his heart (i.e. for the ancient, the seat of consciousness) is taken out and another heart is given to him by a strange power. That new heart is his so long as the other power holds him. Like a dreamer, the man supposes himself to be the onlooker or hearer. He hears a strange unknown voice using his organs of speech, like a plectrum plucking the strings of a lyre. He is in this state of mind because it is as though he has been drugged. The God within declares everything. It is doubtful if a man, when he regains consciousness, can remember what has happened to him. So Montanus declared that God by the Spirit spoke out of him. When Montanus is possessed in that manner he has a ready answer for all those who accuse, but it is God who speaks.

> Neither an angel, nor an apostle,
> But I, the Lord, God the Father, have come.[21]

or

> It is I, the Lord, God the Almighty,
> Descending into a man. . . .[22]

or

> I am the Father and the Son and the Paraclete.[23]

The Spirit speaks in a similar way through Maximilla, Montanus' woman partner. She claimed to be possessed in the same way, and she is reported to have said:

> I am pursued as a wolf among sheep,
> I am no wolf,
> I am the word and the Spirit and the power.[24]

Another remarkable utterance of Maximilla which clearly demonstrates the state of her mind runs:

---

[21] Epiph. *haer.*, XLVIII.xi.164. [22] ibid., XLVIII.xi.3.
[23] Didym. *de trin.*, xli.1.165. [24] Eus. *Hist. Eccl.*, V.xvi f.12.

I was sent by the Lord
As a partaker of this toil
And of the Covenant
And of the promise,
Partaker, proclaimer, and interpreter,
Compelled, willing and not willing
That I may learn
The knowledge of God.[25]

Weinel[26] writing of this passage says: 'At first the prophetess seems to be the speaker, especially because the last words may be related to her, although prophets are not usually sent to learn "the knowledge of God". But "I" is a masculine word here and cannot mean the prophetess. Who is that "I"? The same prophetess says in another utterance which forms an introduction to the prophecy: "Don't hear me, but Christ".'[27] But the contents of the words and the explanation of such a new dogma of the Trinity do not justify us saying that the *I* is Christ. Is another spirit meant? The prophetess seems to be transferring her own feelings to 'the Spirit', calling it 'compelled, willing and not willing'. She perceives her possessed state of mind as compulsion, as being willing and not willing. First 'it' overpowers her from outside and then she gives way to it. The grammatical obscurity has to be explained from the brevity and from the spluttering out of abrupt words by fits and starts. We observe, therefore, that the Montanist leaders all spoke 'under the Spirit'.

We suggested previously that the dream or vision was abnormal or supernormal phenomena attributed to the invasion of human personality by the Spirit. It is significant, but not surprising, that the adherents of Montanism give testimony to experiencing dream phenomena whilst they sleep. Priscilla reported: 'During my sleep, Christ visited me as a woman clad in a splendid garment. He inspired me with wisdom.'[28] Here again is the attempt to revive something that the Church seems to have lost.

The 'form' of these revelations seems to have been the old prophetic form of ecstasy. Eusebius gave an anonymous report: 'He [Montanus] became possessed of a spirit and suddenly began to rave in a kind of ecstatic trance, and to babble in a

---

[25] Epiph. *haer.*, XLVIII.xiii.11.
[26] *Die Wirkungen des Geistes*, pp. 10, 98ff.
[27] Epiph. *haer.* XLVIII.xii.10.
[28] ibid., XLIX.i.9.

jargon, prophesying in a manner contrary to the custom of the Church which had been handed down by tradition from the earliest times.'[29] Here trance, glossolalia, and ecstasy seem to be witnessed almost at one and the same time. Miltiades reports: 'But the false prophet is carried away in a vehement ecstasy accompanied by want of all shame and fear . . . in involuntary madness.' Tertullian gives an account of a prophetic vision: 'We have among us now a sister who has been granted gifts of revelation, which she experiences in church during the Sunday services through ecstatic vision in the Spirit. . . . And after the people have been dismissed at the end of the service it is her custom to relate to us what she has seen. . . . "Among other things," says she, "there was shown to me a soul in bodily form, and it appeared like a spirit; but it was no mere something, void of qualities, but rather a thing which could be grasped, soft and translucent and of ethereal colour, in form at all points human." '[30]

Among the sayings of Montanus, already cited in another connexion, is one which gives his conception of prophecy quite plainly. Man is like a lyre, and the Holy Spirit plays upon him like a plectrum: 'Man sleeps, I (the Spirit) am awake.'

We repeat again that this was no *new* doctrine, it was no heresy. The Church of this century *did* admit the gift of prophecy (at least in theory) for we have seen that Clement, Ignatius, Hermas, Justin Martyr, and Irenæus affirmed their belief in the distribution of charismata. Moreover, this Montanist notion of passivity under spiritual influence was no new doctrine. In A.D. 176 Athenagoras in his *Apology*, speaking of the words of Moses, Isaiah, and Jeremiah, says they '. . . uttered the things with which they were inspired, the Spirit making use of them as a flute-player breathes into a flute'. Justin Martyr expresses the same view with equal clearness. This was the doctrine of the Montanist 'heretics'.

The Montanist leaders were possessed with the idea that the promises in John 14–17 were now being fulfilled in them. The Holy Spirit was now given: He had come in a unique fashion. We must not forget that these men were feeling after something which inherently belongs to the religion of Christ and which authority was endeavouring to destroy. But the Montanist prophecy was not a *return* to the New Testament type of prophecy, through and through. It seems to lack that vitality

[29] *Hist. Eccl.*, xvi.7.   [30] *De anima*, ix.C.210.

MONTANISM: A REVIVAL OF PROPHECY

and balance which make a conquering Christianity. Its type of prophecy seems to have been abnormal and far too narrow. We have seen that they claimed the most absolute divine authority for their revelations. Montanus spoke as the mouthpiece of the Deity, the Lord God Almighty come among men— not an angel nor a messenger but God.[31] The sayings of Maximilla have revealed to us that duality of Divine and human consciousness in her experience. The Montanist prophets obtained their revelations by visions, by conversations with angels and with the Lord and by the actual possession of their minds by the Deity or by the Paraclete; and they delivered them sometimes in the form of glossolalia and at other times in ecstatic but intelligible speech.

They claimed to receive new revelations which applied to the conditions of their time. Tertullian defends them: 'The reason why the Lord sent the Paraclete was that since human mediocrity was unable to take in all things at once, discipline should little by little be directed and ordained and carried on to perfection, by that vicar of the Lord, the Holy Spirit. . . . What then is the Paraclete's administrative office but this: the direction of discipline, the revelation of the scripture, the re-formation of the intellect, the advancement toward "better things"?'[32] Tertullian also declares that it is not the prophetic ecstasy of the Montanists that causes dispute, but their puritanical exercises, etc.[33] It seems that for Tertullian the interest of Montanism lay chiefly in the assurance which the 'New Prophecy' seemed to give, that the Holy Spirit was still teaching in the Church. He is careful to insist that though the movement was a new one, the Spirit was none other than the Paraclete already sent. For Tertullian, and for many adherents, Montanism stood for a recognition of the active presence of the Paraclete in the Church and for a more spiritual and more ascetic type of Church life than the official Churches seemed to offer.[34]

It is most probable that the Church objected to the manner and the professions of the new prophecy rather than to its content. It was a period of caution and growing formality. Ecstatic phenomena had ceased, and had been forgotten and were now believed to be contrary to the tradition of the Church. The abnormal was not expected. Moreover, the Mon-

[31] A. von Harnack, *History of Dogma*, II.97. [32] *De Virg.*, I. [33] *De jejun.*, I.
[34] H. B. Swete, *The Holy Spirit in the Ancient Church*, pp. 79, 83.

tanists set up the ecstatic behaviour of frenzied men and women against and above the growing organization of the Church. Prophecy in the New Testament and Montanist sense, as the immediate deliverance of present divine revelations, could not exist side by side with a fixed rule of faith and a closed canon of divine oracles, guarded by an order of officers established by an external rule of succession. The new prophecy and the only surviving prophecy, was condemned and expelled from the Church as a work of the devil.[35]

We have seen that there was certainly the element of ecstasy in the Apostolic Church, and the prophet known by Paul received visions when 'out of himself'. Yet, in the main, the New Testament prophet was a highly gifted, spiritually developed prophet living on a lofty level of experience.[36] Instead of suppressing his powers and obliterating his reason, instead of sinking to be a 'plucked string', he made himself the organ of an inward Spirit who had become the life of his life, and the power of his faculties. Montanist prophecy seems to have been modelled on heathen oracles and frenzied soothsayings. It was a *return* to types which prevailed in primitive religion. Man is a passive instrument, he imparts nothing of his own; he adds nothing—his personality counts for nothing. This suppression of personality was the weakness of the Montanist revival of prophecy. It was the annihilation of those very faculties through which a personal God could reveal Himself. Another weakness was that the prophecies received were obeyed as a 'new law' instead of being received as spiritual illumination and inspiration, so a collection of 'Paraclete revelation' might form the ultimate law of Christianity. Hence in the Montanist regulations are many laws covering marriage and asceticism. The Montanists, we noted, were 'spirituals' as against ordinary Christians who were called 'psychical' or carnal; they were moving down a dangerous road to spiritual pride and arrogance.

Such is a brief account of this revival of prophecy. The documents from the Montanists are meagre and fragmentary, and one might dismiss the movement as slight. That conclusion is incorrect. The movement was widespread. It swept entire

---

[35] Harnack, op. cit., II.52ff., 95–108. See also Weinel, op cit., pp. 91–101; Eusebius *Hist. Eccl.* V.xvi.7–9.
[36] See Note C, p. 126 *infra*.

communities into fellowship. It emphasized truths which the age needed: it was a powerful protest against a secularized Church. They wanted the Church to be the Church of the Spirit by means of a spiritual man (i.e. the prophet), not the Church which consists of a number of mandatory rulers.

A. V. G. Allen[37] says the question raised by Montanism is 'the eternal question of the ages. On the one hand, administration and order, the well-being of the Church in its collective capacity, the Sacred Book, the oral voice of the Master, the touch of a vanished hand ... some physical chain, as it were, which should bind the generations together, so that they should continue visibly and tangibly to hand on the truth and the life from man to man; and on the other hand, the freedom of the Spirit and the open heaven of revelation ... the vision by which each soul may see Christ for himself through direct and immediate communion with the Spirit of God—that Spirit whose testimony within the soul is the supreme authority and ground of certitude, who takes of the things of Christ and reveals them to men with fresh power and new conviction, who can at any moment authorize initiations of change and progress which yet do not and cannot break the succession of continuous life of the Spirit in the Churches—such were the terms of real issue between Catholicism and Montanism'. This may be an exaggerated suggestion, but it holds truth.

Amid such truth which Montanism asserted there was certainly an error. There were grave dangers in the Montanist emphasis on Spirit-possession. Almost every heresy is born through a sincere and passionate desire for truth, and this movement, unfortunately, developed along the extravagant lines we have noticed. Its original beneficent purpose became wholly lost, and it 'excited no lasting influence over the thought of the Church'.[38] Enthusiasm always carries men to perilous places, but these men sought what men in every age have sought—a religion of the Spirit. Montanism at its best, however, was only a crude and imperfect type of the spirit. Yet, in spite of Swete's assertion about the failure of this movement, Montanism did not really fail. The blood of its martyrs revived faith in the real presence of the Holy Spirit, and its prophetic word about the progress of revelation grew in the hearts of men until a type of the religion of the Spirit could be born,

[37] *Christian Institutions*, p. 103.
[38] H. B. Swete, 'Holy Ghost', *D.C.B.*, III.116.

vivid enough to succeed in bringing contentment to the hungering hearts of men.

It may be that the ecstasy of Montanus and his devotees was deliberately induced, in which case we have no light from Montanus on Pentecost, for there was no artificiality in the Spirit experience of the primitive Church; the only danger of that might have been at Corinth under the influence of the Cephas party. On the other hand, we have suggested that the growing conservatism of the Church caused Montanus to react in an acutely spiritual manner, to receive an outpouring of the Spirit which Montanus believed would descend in great power as upon the community at Pentecost. The resulting spiritual ecstasy would be due to association of ideas with the Spirit, the 'symptom' of whose activity was that very ecstasy. Thus there is reflected in this heresy of the second century something of the atmosphere of the primitive Church.

NOTE C. ADDITIONAL NOTE ON 'PROPHECY IN THE PRIMITIVE CHURCH'[39]

We have seen that with the gift of the Spirit was revived the prophetic consciousness, with accompanying symbolism, ecstasy, vision, etc. If we compare Acts 11^{27}, 12^1, 29^6, and the treatment of the subject of prophecy in 1 Corinthians 12–14, we notice, however, that Paul discriminates between two ideas of prophecy.

In the primitive Church there were men who, by reason of their possession of the gift of prophecy, played an important part in the edification of believers. Indeed, they stood so near to the apostles in the quality of their service that Paul describes the Church as 'being built upon the foundation of the apostles and prophets' (Ephesians 2^{20}). We have seen that 'prophet' stood for a gift rather than an office, and men of that type would be found in every local Church.

The earlier New Testament conception of prophecy was that of prediction (Acts $11^{27f.}$, 21^{11}). Later, however, to a much greater extent it represented what we should call 'inspired preaching'. The themes dealt with would be some phase of Christian duty,[40] the nature of the unseen world, or the Divine

---

[39] See Rudolf Otto, *The Kingdom of God and the Son of Man*, pp. 357–67.

[40] I Corinthians 7^{40}: 'And I think that I also have the Spirit of God', may suggest that Paul was controverting the ideas which have been put forward in the Corinthian Church on marriage by 'prophets' who claimed to be speaking under the influence of the Spirit. A. Lewis Humphries, *The Holy Spirit in Faith and Experience*, p. 208, n.1.

programme for the future, or some other theme which was revealed.[41]

The prophet was distinguished from the ordinary teacher by the fact that the prophet knew that a revelation had been given to him either directly or through a vision by the Spirit whose mouthpiece he was then called to be. Both the teacher and prophet aimed to instruct their hearers, but the teacher's message came rather through personal study and reflection—there was more of the human teacher in it (Acts 10^{11-16}, 16^9, 18^9, 22^{17-21}, $27^{23\text{ff.}}$).

Moreover, prophesying differed from glossolalia in that it was always intelligible to both speaker and hearers. The stimulation of prophecy involved no loss of mental control. At the same time, the utterances of the prophets were not regarded as immune from criticism. The subjects with which they dealt were often speculative in character, which afforded play, probably unconsciously, for merely human fancy. Hence there were divided opinions about prophesying. Some churches might have been disposed to repress manifestations of the spirit in their worship. The Church of Thessalonica was one such place which tended to think lightly on the utterances of these 'inspired preachers'. So Paul has to charge its members, 'Quench not the Spirit . . . despise not prophesyings', though he adds a command to employ a wise discrimination: 'prove all things; hold fast to that which is good . . .' (1 Thessalonians 5^{19-22}).[42]

Paul laid down as one of the regulations of worship at Corinth that not more than two or three prophets were to speak in one meeting (1 Corinthians $14^{29\text{f.}}$)[43] and when they had done so the rest of the Church, probably by means of informal discussion, was to pass judgement on the teaching which had been given.

In this way prophesying was restrained from extravagance. It was required to satisfy the common sense and intelligence of

[41] cf. *Revelation* in New Testament, an example of vision-prophecy.

[42] ἀπὸ παντὸς εἴδους πονηροῦ ἀπέχεσθε, not 'every appearance of evil', but 'every evil kind or species'—here, of spiritual phenomena. Paul speaks of διακρίσεις πνευμάτων, 'discernment of spirits', i.e. discrimination of spiritual phenomena (1 Corinthians 12^{10}). Cf. A. Lewis Humphries, *The Holy Spirit in Faith and Experience*, p. 209, n.1.

[43] Paul also seems to direct that if a 'prophet' has a revelation while the meeting is in progress, any other 'prophet' who may be speaking at the moment must sit down and make way for the new revelation. A doctrinal test was also imposed on prophesying (1 Corinthians 12^3; 1 John 4^2).

the Christian community. Later on, the Church, because it had at times been deceived by those who had pretended to speak in the name of God, applied other tests to the professed 'prophet', e.g. the absence of self-seeking, the prophet's practice in comparison with his teaching, his Christlikeness; in this manner, the men claiming the gift of prophecy visiting the local Church were sifted.[44]

[44] cf. the *Didache*—A visiting prophet was not to stay more than two days, he must only have hospitality. 'Let him take nothing but bread . . . if he ask money he is a false prophet . . . not everyone that speaketh in spirit is a prophet, but only if he have the ways of the Lord . . . by their ways shall be known the false prophet and the prophet. Every prophet that teacheth the truth, if he doeth not the things that he teacheth, is a false prophet' (*Doctrina Apost.*). Cited by H. Bettenson, *Documents of the Christian Church*, pp. 91f.

CHAPTER ELEVEN

Conclusion: The Invasion of the Spirit

WE HAVE seen how abnormal and supernormal phenomena in the religious life of the Old Testament were attributed to the invasion of human personality by an outside power—the Spirit of God. Sometimes a dream was the vehicle of that possession. But at all stages of historical development the prophet was the clearest expression in this life of the Spirit-possessed man, so that the New Testament era heralded above all a revival of prophecy. The Pentecost experiences meant the recapturing of this prophetic consciousness—but now the experience was available for *all*—'to you and your children'. One of the great signs of possession by the Spirit we have seen was 'glossolalia'. This ecstasy we have remarked was an element in the Montanist movement. In conclusion we may take a rapid survey of religious history and we shall discover many analogies to light up the nature of this Invasion of the Spirit which we have seen expressed in the Pentecost experience.

Leaders of new religious movements seem to have been specially liable to the Spirit manifestations: this may have been partly because of their absorbing interest in religion and partly also because, as Prof. James suggests, in them a superior intellect and psychopathic temperament coalesced.[1] Men like Luther, Bernard of Clairvaux, St Francis of Assisi, and Loyola, all had abnormal and supernormal spiritual experiences. We have already referred to Montanism. The Camisards of France revealed an intensified religious experience under the fierce pressure of persecution.

During the rising of the seventeenth century many of the Protestants of Languedoc went into ecstasy which infected people of all ages. 'They heard supernatural voices. They spoke with tongues. Children of the tenderest years were the subjects of most extraordinary manifestations. Quite uneducated persons gave utterance when "seized by the Spirit" to prophecies in purest French.' Here are hints of the Pentecost atmosphere.

[1] W. James, *Varieties of Religious Experience*, pp. 23, 478.

The spiritual atmosphere of the *Journal* of George Fox is very suggestive in this connexion. 'It was opened unto me by the eternal light and power, and I saw clearly therein all that was done, and to be done, in and by Christ.' Fox attended a large meeting, and 'the Lord opened my mouth . . . and the power of the Lord was over them all. . . . I saw the harvest white, and the seed of God lying thick in the ground. . . .' Or again: 'The Lord's power began to shake them.' The people 'wait to feel the Lord's power and spirit in themselves'. At Carlisle, as Fox was speaking, 'the power of the Lord was dreadful amongst them in the steeple-house so that the people trembled and shook and they thought the steeple-house shook; and some of them feared it would fall down on their heads'.[2] Bushnell[3] reports instances of glossolalia, of the prophetic gift, and of significant vision which had come under his own observation. He also explains the recurrence of these abnormal phenomena in the life of the Church as due to periodic enlargements of activity on the part of the Holy Spirit—be this as it may, the history of religion shows that to an impressive degree this survival or revival of these spiritual phenomena has actually taken place.

In the history of the Methodist Revival one finds singular manifestations of abnormality attached to the early history of nearly all the Methodist Churches. In his *Journal* John Wesley refers to these strange features again and again. Nothing akin to glossolalia[4] is described by Wesley, but something astonishingly near must frequently have appeared in Methodism in many a fervent love-feast and prayer meeting. Wesley's *Journal*[5] contains detailed descriptions of experiences ranging from instantaneous conversion followed by immediate elation and joy, to pathological tortures, both mental and physical, some of which culminated in permanent mental derangement. Sydney G. Dimond has examined almost all the cases enumerated from 1739 to 1743 and makes interesting observations concerning the phenomena.[6] The peculiar manifestations recorded frequently in the second and third volumes of Wesley's *Journal*

[2] Cited by P. G. S. Hopwood, *The Religious Experience of the Primitive Church*, pp. 155f.

[3] *Nature and the Supernatural*, pp. 327-36. See also J. B. Pratt, *The Religious Consciousness*, pp. 184-94.

[4] Extreme physical effects, such as 'barking', jerks, etc., which have been observed in other revivals, are absent from the Methodist records. See F. M. Davenport, *Primitive Traits in Religious Revivals*, pp. 70-80.

[5] II.331, 379, 385.

[6] *Psychology of the Methodist Revival*, ad loc., especially Chap. 6.

CONCLUSION: THE INVASION OF THE SPIRIT 131

include convulsive tearings, violent trembling, groaning, strong cries, and tears, etc. The following are typical examples: 'I was desired to step thence to a neighbouring house . . . a young woman came in all in tears, and deep anguish of spirit . . . she now found the Spirit of God was departed from her. We began to pray, and she cried out, "He is come! He is come! . . ." Just as we rose from giving thanks, another person reeled four or five steps, and then dropped down. . . .'[7] The night previous, John Haydon, a weaver, had been affected. He was reading a sermon, 'Salvation by Faith'. 'In reading the last page he changed colour, fell off his chair, and began screaming terribly, and beating himself against the ground.'[8] Under date 6th August 1759, Wesley tells of conversation 'with Ann Thorn and two others, who had been several times in trances. What they all agreed in was that when they went away, as they termed it, it was always at the time they were fullest of the love of God. . . .'[9]

It appears that John Wesley interpreted these peculiar manifestations as signs. 'Perhaps it might be because of the hardness of our hearts, unready to receive anything unless we see it with our eyes and hear it with our ears, that God, in tender condescension to our weakness, suffered so many outward signs of the very time when He wrought this inward change to be seen and heard among us.'[10] Some suggest that Wesley encouraged these signs.[11] Whatever may be our judgement upon that, it is certain that Wesley revised his opinion as to the significance and as to the cause of these symptoms. He suggested in his later ministry that they might be extravagances,[12] and was convinced that it was satanic or demon influence that was attacking the penitent coming to Christ.[13] The extreme physical disturbances are a diminishing quantity, and rarely appear in any part of the country after the year 1743. Moreover, Wesley could not tolerate the hysterical behaviour of the Camisards, whom he met from time to time in various parts of England.[14]

In early Primitive Methodism trance-phenomena gathered around James Crawfoot, a sort of religious mystic dwelling in

[7] *Journal*, II.188–9. See note, p. 189.
[8] ibid., II.189–91. Also see II.240, 254, 289; III.60–9; and L. Tyerman, *Life and Times of John Wesley*, I.255–68.
[9] *Journal*, IV.344. [10] ibid., II.202; *Works*, I.184. See L. Tyerman, op. cit., I.267.
[11] *Journal*, III.51. [12] ibid., VII.153. [13] ibid., III.69.
[14] ibid., II.136, 226; VII.153; see Sydney G. Dimond, op. cit., pp. 135f.

Delamere Forest, and the circle which he influenced (chiefly in the years 1810–12). Hugh Bourne witnessed the phenomena and believed in their genuineness. Later on Hugh Bourne gave his sober judgement upon such manifestations.[15]

Among the Quaker community there were many who had visions and 'openings' and revelations. The Irvingite movement arose in the third decade of the nineteenth century from the insistence that the Spirit's remarkable gifts, as manifested at Pentecost and in the Apostolic Church, were a permanent possession of the Church withheld because of the unfaithfulness of Christian believers. The gift of 'tongues' is said to have been freely exercised among the followers of Edward Irving, and there are reports of deliberate attempts to excite artificially the gift at Ashton-under-Lyne.[16] Irving made a deliberate attempt to found a Church completely after the Apostolic pattern, and it would appear that the 'gifts' were mechanical and purposed products. The abnormal and supernormal phenomena were manufactured. This cannot be said of the gift of 'tongues' which Erskine of Linlathen reports as having been exercised by the two Macdonalds of Port Glasgow. They were men of unimpeachable character, men of calmness and balanced understanding. 'Yet associated with them was not only a power of healing the sick but also occasional lapses into ecstatic utterances.'[17]

Mary Campbell lay sick at Fernicarry. One Sunday evening in March 1830 whilst visiting friends were praying, Mary 'suddenly, as if possessed by a superhuman strength . . . broke forth, speaking in an unknown tongue, in loud ecstatic utterances for more than an hour'.[18] At about the same time friends living at Port Glasgow saw their sister, Margaret, healed. They immediately informed Mary Campbell of this healing, writing: 'Faith in His name has given her soundness in the presence of us all. . . . Mary . . . hear God's voice to you also, "Rise up and walk". . . .' Mary, referring to this incident, writes: 'I had scarcely read the first page when I became quite overpowered and laid it aside . . . but I had no rest in my spirit until I took it up again and began to read. As I read, every word came with power, but when I came to the command to rise, it came home with new power . . . it was felt to be indeed the voice of Christ

---

[15] See his *Journal*, 4th October 1828, in reference to the revival at Prees.
[16] See *Daily News*, 21st February 1911.
[17] A. Lewis Humphries, *The Holy Spirit in Faith and Experience*, p. 230.
[18] W. Hanna, *Letters of Thomas Erskine*, I.176.

CONCLUSION: THE INVASION OF THE SPIRIT

... it was such a voice of power as could not be resisted....'[19]

After her recovery, Mary Campbell lived at Helensburgh, where frequent religious meetings were held. To the speaking with tongues was added writing with unknown tongues. When the moment of inspiration came, Mary seized the pen, and with a rapidity 'like lightning' covered sheets of paper with characters believed to be letters and words. The gift of prophecy was also largely exercised, 'a gift not to be confounded with foretelling of future events or ordinary teaching, but consisting in inspired exalted utterances, opening up some obscure passage of scripture'.[20] The area of manifestation was enlarged, and interest was shown in all parts of England, Scotland, and Ireland.[21] The following quotation from the *Edinburgh Review* is the report of a solicitor who witnessed these phenomena.

'These persons, while uttering the unknown sounds, as also while speaking in the Spirit in their own language, have every appearance of being under supernatural direction. The manner and voice are (speaking generally) different from what they are at other times, and on ordinary occasions. This difference does not consist merely in the peculiar solemnity and fervour of manner (which they possess) but their whole deportment gives an impression, not to be conveyed in words, that their organs are made use of by supernatural power.... They declare that their organs of speech are made use of by the Spirit of God, and that they utter that which is given to them, and not the expressions of their own conceptions, or their own intention....'[22]

We have referred at length to these phenomena reported by the Macdonalds and Erskine because these are probably the most careful observations we have regarding glossolalia in modern times. So we find the following interesting note in Hanna's *Letters of Thomas Erskine*. He mentions that glossolalia seems to have impressed Mr Erskine and Mr Irving in the same manner and to the same effect. 'The languages', says Mr Erskine, reporting their effect upon his ear, 'are distinct, well-inflected, well-compacted languages; they are not random collections of sounds; they are composed of words of various length, with the

---

[19] W. Hanna, *Letters of Thomas Erskine*, p. 179, quoted from *A Vindication of the Religion of the Land*, by the Rev. A. Robertson, pp. 251, 254.

[20] W. Hanna, op. cit., p. 179.   [21] ibid., pp. 180f.

[22] 'Pretended Miracles', Irving, Scott, and Erskine, First Article in No. 106 of the *Edinburgh Review* (June 1831), quoted by W. Hanna, op. cit., p. 181.

natural variety, and yet possessing that commonness of character which marks them to be one distinct language. I have heard many people speak gibberish, but this is not gibberish, it is decidedly well-compacted language.' Mr Irving's report is similar. He says: 'The whole utterance, from the beginning to the ending of it, is with a power and a strength and fullness, and sometimes rapidity of voice, altogether different from that of the persons' ordinary utterance in any mood: and I would say, both in its form and in its effects upon a simple mind, quite supernatural. There is a power in the voice to thrill the heart and overawe the spirit . . . there is a march and a majesty and a sustained grandeur in the voice, which I have never heard even a resemblance to. It is mere abandonment to all truth to call it a screaming or crying; it is the most majestic and divine utterance which I have ever heard, some parts of which I never heard equalled, and no part of it surpassed, but the finest execution of genius and art exhibited at the oratorios in the concerts of ancient music.'[23]

There is a third witness who had many opportunities of seeing these strange phenomena, Archibald M'Kerrell, and he says: 'The exhibition of the gift transcends all power of description. . . . A previous silence and an extraordinary change of countenance will generally intimate to others its approach, it will then occur that they will clutch the nearest friend by the hand with an iron grasp, and speak out in the tongue, part of the time with the eyes closed, and then opened with the most intensely searching and fixed look. . . . The deportment of the speaker is extraordinary in the last degree; the countenance receives a dignity and a ravishment of expression superhuman; all traces of a self-agent are fled from the features; the tone of voice is quite unearthly. You stand in the immediate presence of God.' Mr M'Kerrell wrote down some of the utterances; the following are specimens: '*O Pinitos, Elelastino Halimangitos Dantita, Hampoothri, Farimi, Aristos Eliampros.*'[24]

So we could continue collecting historical evidence which shows that in the historical development of the Church there have been abnormal and supernormal phenomena attributed to the invasion of human personality by the Spirit of God. From Apostolic days through the winding way of history to the witness of the Elim tabernacle hidden away in the mean

[23] W. Hanna, op. cit., p. 392.
[24] *An Apology for the Gift of Tongues*, pp. 10, 11; quoted by W. Hanna, op. cit., p. 393.

CONCLUSION: THE INVASION OF THE SPIRIT

streets of almost every city, there are found those who point to the abnormal and supernormal manifestations and say: 'There is the mark of the Spirit.'

As we conclude our study of the gift of the Spirit we do well to remind ourselves that the mark of the Spirit is not merely in some physical expression as in glossolalia; or strange psychic experience like the trance—the greatest mark is that the Invasion of the Spirit produces *character* which is supernormal. We have seen that the conception of the Spirit passed over into Christianity from the Old Testament. When the Spirit comes, wisdom and strength come from God. The invasion of the Spirit is an invasion which uplifts and fortifies the will, so that men can yield themselves unreservedly to God's service. It is this which makes for righteousness, holiness, and fellowship with God. The prophetic frenzy was explained by reference to this supernatural possession, so when the prophet stood out not merely as an ecstatic, but as an interpreter of God's will, his messages were still attributed to possession by the Spirit.

Jesus says little about the Spirit, probably because His attitude to God was one of direct and personal trust, and He required no intermediary, but to help His followers He reminded them of 'the promise'. So in consequence of the outbreak of strange phenomena, the followers who were 'waiting for the promise' could not but attribute such phenomena to some power from the invisible world. What could it be but the Spirit? The promise had been fulfilled! The Church always related the Spirit experience to Christ. The Spirit was only operative in the community which believed in Him. The action of the Spirit, as already suggested, was recognized once only in the ecstatic phenomena, but soon it was extended to *all* the new energies which marked the Church and the Christian's life in society. The invasion of the Spirit was the power and drive of the Christian New Order. Disciples of Christ did indeed become different men, possessing higher capacities of insight and courage and endurance; 'it was through the action of the Spirit that the earthly nature was transformed and wrought into affinity to the nature of Christ.' It was through the activity of the Spirit that the Kingdom of God would be brought in.

Doubtless we should now explain in terms of psychology many of those phenomena which excited the marvel of the Early Church, but it is impossible to explain merely in terms of psychology the new source of power which the Early Church described as the gift of the Spirit. The Christians were conscious that something new and wonderful had entered into their lives. They knew themselves in contact with a higher world—with forces that were manifestly of God. It is this conviction that gives meaning to Christianity, and we do not dispose of it when we attempt to define it in psychological or philosophical phrases that might only cover up our ignorance. Life had really come at Pentecost. The touch of the Spirit had quickened in the assembled disciples' Life—Life which was unmistakable in its power and quality, Life which (although, as we have seen, emphasis was at first laid on its psycho-physical concomitants) proved its existence and its quality by its fruit in the sphere of conduct and character.[25] William James calls this, 'that touch of explosive intensity'.

The believers in the New Testament and in the Early Church were convinced that the Holy Spirit was the real dynamic of the Christian religion. There are historic facts and mental processes which the Spirit uses, but these facts and conceptions are but useful pivots of power and not the power itself. The power itself is the energizing will of the Spirit. The gift of the Spirit is that truth which makes possible the complete redemption of the world's black soul.[26] The crucial declaration of the New Testament is that the soul, or personality, of any man can be utterly transformed by the gift of the Spirit. All human needs are met; the warfare of the flesh is overcome (Galatians 5^{17}); the fruit of the Spirit is produced ($5^{22f.}$); and victory over the devil and the world is accomplished. So then, the objective dynamic of Christian ethics is the Holy Spirit, or God exerting moral and creative power. We must remind ourselves again that 'the Spirit is not simply the immanent Spirit of God, as that is generally viewed. Its character is revealed and its power acts through Jesus. A great moral activity of God has been manifested in the life and death of Jesus, which makes the beginning of specific ethical Christian experience possible. . . .'[27]

The invasion of the Spirit, then, is the 'Uprush of Life'[28] that touches all life because it renews all life. There can be no divorce between Christian experience and Christian ethics. One cannot have the ethics of Christ and be disloyal to the

[25] C. A. Scott, *The Fellowship of the Spirit*, pp. 49f.
[26] O. A. Curtis, *The Christian Faith*, p. 117.
[27] Donald Mackenzie, Article, 'Ethics and Morality', *Encyclopædia of Religion and Ethics*, V.469.
[28] C. A. Scott, op. cit., Chap. 3.

CONCLUSION: THE INVASION OF THE SPIRIT

fellowship of Christ. All the moral precepts of Jesus flow from a religious principle. The ideal picture of human life for Jesus is a picture of life in the Kingdom of God on earth, 'life as it may be lived by men who acknowledge one supreme loyalty, in whose hearts one supreme passion burns'.[29] The Spirit operates only in those who are members of that Kingdom—or in other words the Spirit operates solely within the Church. It is the work of the Spirit to integrate men into that New Society. The Society called into existence by the Spirit must have precedence over every other, first because of its potential universality and then because of the all-inclusive character of its goal. Nothing that belongs to the true welfare of men lies outside its scope, or beyond the reach of its power. This Fellowship of the Spirit has the characteristic of universality, because the sole condition of entering is a right relation to God through Jesus Christ. Distinctions of organization, like those of race, sex, or social standing are irrelevant in the Fellowship of the Spirit.[30] The gift of the Spirit is the distinguishing feature of the Christian religion.[31]

The gift of the Spirit is thus intimately related to the New Testament idea of the perfect life.

We have observed that the highest thought about the gift of the Spirit is expressed in the conception that the gift is given not to create abnormal physical phenomena but so that ordinary men and women might produce character that is supernormal. The Christian disciple is called to live Christ's kind of life. He must 'be perfect' as his 'Father who is in heaven is perfect' (Matthew 5^{48}): Jesus prayed for that kind of perfection (John 17^{20-3}). Paul's prayers are burdened with the same plea (1 Thessalonians 5^{23}). That kind of life is a human impossibility. Our experience declares that holiness, the life of perfect love, that kind of Christian perfection, is never artificially produced. It is a gift. John Wesley is surely correct when he interprets the mind of the New Testament writers about the gift of the Spirit as saying that the Holy Spirit is peculiarly associated with this sanctification of life. He says that the Spirit is responsible for 'the conversion and entire sanctification of our hearts and lives. . . . The title "holy" applied to the Spirit of God does not only denote that He is

---

[29] T. W. Manson, *The Teaching of Jesus*, Chap. 9.
[30] C. A. Scott, op. cit., pp. 226f.
[31] S. Chadwick, *The Way to Pentecost*, p. 117.

holy in His own nature, but that He makes us so; that He is the great fountain of holiness to His Church; the Spirit from whence flows all the grace and virtue. . . .'[32]

The Wesleys, however, never claimed that what happened to the spiritually impotent members of the Holy Club at Oxford was the experience of another Pentecost. It was Pentecostal but not Pentecost. Something was done on the first Whit-Sunday that cannot be repeated. No Pentecostal claims are made for the new Methodist community. What were claimed and expected were new and repeated infusions of the Spirit, a future pouring out of the Holy Ghost which would give to those who have the form of religion, its power. Even then there is little sense, if any, of a corporate, as distinct from an individual, empowering. So Wesley wrote:

> Our glorified Head
> His Spirit hath shed,
> With His people to stay,
> And never again will He take Him away.[33]

There is nothing for which we can be more grateful than the witness of the Wesleys to the personal operations of the Holy Spirit. They did not look for physical signs, but for spiritual graces: 'the vivid realization in the hearts of their people of the living Christ through the Spirit's power and witness: the experience of thousands of individuals that the Holy Spirit was not the special possession of prophet, priest, or ecclesiastical organization, but the Divine gift to all flesh, so that multitudes saw visions and dreamt dreams'.[34] If any verse sums up the Wesleys' thought on this subject, it is the verse that has been sung with deep fervour and with rich and abiding results:

> Refining Fire, go through my heart,
> Illuminate my soul;
> Scatter Thy life through every part,
> And sanctify the whole.[35]

---

[32] Wesley, *Works*, VII.485f. See also *Methodist Hymn Book* (1933), Nos. 275, 277, 278, 280, 284, 294, 299; 547, 548, 549, 553, 554, 555, 557, 560, 568⁴, 274; cf. H. Scougal, *Life of God in the Soul of Man*, p. 9, W. Marshall, *The Gospel-Mystery of Sanctification*, p. 127.
[33] *M.H.B.* (1933), No. 278⁴.
[34] J. E. Rattenbury, *The Evangelical Doctrine of Charles Wesley's Hymns*, pp. 186f.
[35] *M.H.B.*, No. 387⁶.

CONCLUSION: THE INVASION OF THE SPIRIT 139

Paul's doctrine of the believer's mystic indwelling in Christ, and Christ's in the believer, we can link up with this gift of the Spirit. It is the contrast between 'having a life *alongside* God, and having life *in* God'. The change of the preposition in the Johannine discourses about the Spirit is probably rich in meaning—'abideth *with* you, and shall be *in* you' (John 14⁷).[36] All supernormal conduct and service and character was a result of this indwelling (Acts 2⁴, 4³¹, 6³,⁵, 7⁵⁵, 9³¹). It is a gift for ordinary people (Acts 4³¹, 13⁵²); almost every Christian grace is associated with the Spirit (Acts 6⁵, 9³¹, 10³⁸, 11²⁴, 13⁵²). The gift is not a luxury for the few, nor is it for special occasions; it is a gift for the whole business of living. We read that Stephen was permanently full of the Spirit ($ὑπάρχων\ δὲ\ πλήρης$, Acts 7⁵⁵) and we may say that such an experience is possible for all, for God is pledged to give the Holy Spirit to them that ask Him (Luke 11¹³).

Supernormal service and conduct and living, then, for the Christian disciple, is only possible as men are invaded by the Spirit, but the Spirit is *given*. The Spirit is not to be strained after. Those who have strained after holiness have been weary and disappointed. The gift is received, and the gift is a *supernatural* gift. Effectiveness goes when this gift is absent. The apostles were ordinary men—but they had known Pentecost. They turned the world upside down (Acts 17⁶).

It can happen again to our world that is bruised, bowed down, and bleeding, because of sin and circumstance. Commerce can be redeemed, the twist can be taken out of business life, international dishonesties can go, every detail of international and domestic relationships can be totally renewed—but not by human achievement alone! Such a colossal redemption is abnormal and supernormal. The Christian declares that we need a power to descend from the invisible world to lift us—that is the power of the Spirit. The Old Faith is vitally related to the New Order. Man cannot build Jerusalem in this green and pleasant land. As Dr J. Whale[37] concludes, 'the political science of twenty-one civilizations has never created a just society, let alone a perfect one. The New Jerusalem must come down out of heaven from God Himself. This means that at the end of all things it is goodness that matters, the personal integrity of redeemed and dedicated people. Goodness means

---

[36] W. E. Sangster, *The Path to Perfection*, p. 195.
[37] J. Whale, *The Old Faith and the New Order*, pp. 15f.

a quality of life springing from goodwill which, because it has been set free from that fatal egocentricity which underlies all moral failure, is able to rise to a new level of moral competence.' This is the achievement of the Spirit as conceived by the New Testament. The power of the Spirit will lead toward a grand and glorious renewal. The New Testament conceives of life in the Spirit as normal Christianity. The gift of the Spirit is for all. It is given to those who are Christ's followers unconditionally, who are His without reserve. This gift is the Living Flame whose possession makes a man 'more than conqueror'. It is the 'sacred fire' which kindles that blazing passion for social righteousness and that warm, crusading love, which are the distinctive marks of those who are Christ's men, and Christ's alone.

BIBLIOGRAPHY

Allen, A. V. G., *Christian Institutions*.
Barrett, C. K., *The Holy Spirit and the Gospel Tradition*.
Barth, K., *Der Römerbrief*.
Bettenson, H., *Documents of the Christian Church*.
Beyer, H. W., 'Apostelgeschichte' (*Das Neue Testament Deutsch*).
Blau, L., *Das Altjüdische Zauberwesen*.
Borchert, Otto, *The Original Jesus*.
Bousset, W., *Die Religion des Judentums im neutest. Zeitalter*.
Buechsel, F., *Der Geist Gottes*.
Bushnell, H., *Nature and the Supernatural*.
Butterfield, Herbert, *Christianity in European History*.
Butterworth, G. W., *Spiritualism and Religion*.
Canaan, T., *Dämonenglaube im Lande der Bibel*.
Casson, Stanley, *The Discovery of Man*.
Chadwick, S., *The Way to Pentecost*.
Curtis, O. A., *The Christian Faith*.
Cutten, G., *Speaking with Tongues*.
Davenport, F. M., *Primitive Traits in Religious Revivals*.
Davidson, A. B., 'Prophecy and Prophets' (*H.D.B.*, Vol. IV).
Davidson, W. T., *The Indwelling Spirit*.
Davies, T. W., *Magic, Divination and Demonology*.
Denney, James, 'Holy Spirit' (*D.C.G.*, I).
De Soyres, *Montanism and the Primitive Church*.
Dillman, C. F. A., *Handbuch der alttestament lichen Theologie*.
Dimond, Sydney G., *Psychology of the Methodist Revival*.
Dix, G., *The Apostolic Tradition*.
Duhm, H., *Die bösen Geister im Alten Testament*.
Dupont-Sommer, A., *The Dead Sea Scrolls*.
Findlay, J. A., *The Acts of the Apostles (Commentary)*.
Flew, R. Newton, *The Idea of Perfection*.
Galloway, G., *The Philosophy of Religion*.
Glover, T. R., *Paul of Tarsus*.
Guillaume, A., *Prophecy and Divination*.
Gwatkin, H. M., *Selections from Early Christian Writers*.
Hanna, W., *Letters of Thomas Erskine*.
Harnack, A. von, *History of Dogma*, Vol. II.
Hastings, J., *Dictionary of Christ and the Gospels*.
Hastings, J., *Dictionary of the Bible*.
Hopwood, P. G. S., *The Religious Experience of the Primitive Church*.
Hoyle, R. Birch, *The Holy Spirit in St Paul*.
Humphries, A. Lewis, *The Holy Spirit in Faith and Experience*.
Inge, Dean, *Christian Mysticism*.
Jackson, Foakes and Lake, *The Beginnings of Christianity*, Vols. I, V.
James, W., *Varieties of Religious Experience*.
Janet, Pierre, *Major Symptoms of Hysteria*.

BIBLIOGRAPHY

Jones, Rufus M., *Studies in Mystical Religion*.
Karsten, R., *The Origins of Religion*.
Knight, Harold, *The Hebrew Prophetic Consciousness*.
Labriolle, P. de, *La Crise Montaniste*.
Labriolle, P. de, *Les Sources de l'histoire de Montanisme*.
Langton, Edward, *Essentials of Demonology*.
Langton, Edward, *Good and Evil Spirits*.
Lehmann, E., *Aberglaube und Zauberei*.
Lévy-Bruhl, L., *Primitive Mentality*.
Liddell and Scott, *Greek-English Lexicon*.
Lietzmann, H., *Die Geschichte der Alten Kirche*.
Lietzmann, H., *Handbuch zum Neuen Testament*.
Lods, A., *Israel*.
Lods, A., *The Prophets and the Rise of Judaism*.
Lofthouse, W. F., *Israel after the Exile*, Clarendon Bible, IV.
Macdonald, A. J., *The Holy Spirit*.
Macdonald, A. J., *The Interpreter Spirit and Human Life*.
Mackenzie, Donald, 'Ethics and Morality' (*E.R.E.*).
Major, Manson and Wright, *The Mission and Message of Jesus*.
Manson, T. W., *St Paul in Ephesus* (3), *Corinthian Correspondence*. (Bulletin of J. Rylands Library).
Manson, T. W., *The Teaching of Jesus*.
Marcus, R., *Law in the Apocrypha*.
Marshall, W., *The Gospel-Mystery of Sanctification*.
Meyer, E., *Ursprung und Anfänge des Christentums*.
Michaëlis, Wilhelm, *Das neue Testament, II*.
Montgomery, A., *Incantation Texts from Nippur*.
Moore, G. F., *Judaism*.
Oesterreich, T. K., *Possession, Demoniacal and Other*.
Otto, Rudolf, *The Kingdom of God and the Son of Man*.
Pratt, J. B., *The Religious Consciousness*.
Rackham, R. B., *Acts*, Westminster Commentary.
Rattenbury, J. E., *The Evangelical Doctrine of Charles Wesley's Hymns*.
Rees, T., *The Holy Spirit*.
Reitzenstein, R., *Die hellenistischen Mysterienreligionen nach ihren Grundgedanken und Wirkungen*.
Robinson, H. W., *Redemption and Revelation*.
Robinson, H. W., *The Religious Ideas of the Old Testament*.
Robinson, T. H., *Prophecy and the Prophets*.
Sangster, W. E., *The Path to Perfection*.
Schmidt, W., *Gnostiche Schriften in coptischen Sprache*.
Scott, C. Anderson, *The Fellowship of the Spirit*.
Scott, E. F., *The Spirit in the New Testament*.
Scougal, H., *Life of God in the Soul of Man*.
Selwyn, E. G., *The Christian Prophets*.
Smith, W. Robertson, *Religion of the Semites*.
Snaith, Norman H., *The Distinctive Ideas of the Old Testament*.
Snaith, Norman H., *The Doctrine of the Holy Spirit*.
Stewart, J. S., *A Faith to Proclaim*.
Strack, H. L., and Billerbeck, P., *Kommentar zum Neuen Testament*.

Summers, M., *The History of Witchcraft and Demonology*.
Swete, H. B., *The Holy Spirit in the Ancient Church*.
Swete, H. B., *The Holy Spirit in the New Testament*.
Taylor, V., H. Roberts, H. Watkin-Jones, N. Snaith, *The Doctrine of the Holy Spirit* (Headingley Lectures).
Thomas, W. H. G., *The Holy Spirit of God*.
Tyerman, L., *Life and Times of John Wesley*, Vol. I.
Volz, P., *Der Geist Gottes*.
Walker, Dawson, *The Gift of Tongues*.
Walker, T., *Hebrew Religion between the Testaments*.
Wardle, W. L., *The History and Religion of Israel*, Clarendon Bible, I.
Weinel, H., *Die Wirkungen des Geistes und der Geister*.
Weiss, J., *The History of Primitive Christianity*.
Wesley, J., *Journal*.
Wesley, J., *Letters*.
Wesley, J., *Works*.
Whale, J., *The Old Faith and the New Order*.
Winstanley, E. W., *Spirit in the New Testament*.
Wood, I. F., *The Spirit of God in Biblical Literature*.

Dictionaries and Encyclopædias

The Apocrypha and Pseudepigrapha of the Old Testament (ed. R. H. Charles).
Dictionary of the Bible (ed. J. Hastings) (H.D.B.).
Dictionary of Christ and the Gospels (ed. J. Hastings) (D.C.G.).
Encyclopædia of Religion and Ethics (ed. J. Hastings) (E.R.E.).
The Jewish Encyclopædia (ed. Isidore Singer).

Index of Old Testament Passages

Genesis
1^2	43
2^7	39
2^{28}	45
3	36
$15^{1f., 12f.}$	5
15^{17}	36
20^3	3
28^{12}	4
31^{24}	4
35^4	55
$37^{5, 9}$	4
40	4
40^8	45
41	4
$41^{15f.}$	4
41^{16}	45
41^{25}	4
41^{32}	4
41^{38}	45

Exodus
3^2	36
$4^{15f.}$	12
7^1	11
$13^{9f.}$	55
$13^{21f.}$	36
15	41
$15^{20f.}$	14
16	55
19	50
19^{16}	36, 87
19^{19}	88
20^{18}	88
23^9	38
24^3	88
35^{31}	45

Numbers
5^{14}	40
$11^{16f.}$	45
11^{29}	49
12^{2-15}	14
$12^{6f.}$	5
22^{4-16}	14
24^{13}	48

Deuteronomy
6^8	55
11^{18}	55
13^{3-4}	5
$18^{15ff.}$	47

Judges
3^{10}	44
$4-5$	14
5^4	36
6^{34}	44
7^{13}	4
9^{23}	39, 73
14^6	40, 44
14^{19}	44
15^{14}	39, 40, 44

I Samuel
2^{16}	38
$3^{1, 3f.}$	5
$9^{1ff.}$	12, 13
9^9	13
$9^{15f.}$	12
10^5	14, 27
$10^{6, 9}$	13, 28
10^{10}	13
16^{13}	44
18^{10}	39, 73
$19^{20, 24}$	13
20^4	38
$28^{6, 13}$	5

II Samuel
$7^{4ff.}$	5
23^1	15

I Kings
$3^{5, 15}$	4
8^{10}	36
17^{22}	38
18^{12}	40
$18^{20ff.}$	13
$18^{25f., 46}$	14
$19^{11f.}$	32
20^{35-43}	15
22^{5-28}	13, 15, 73

II Kings
2^{16}	40
3^{15}	13
3^{16}	40
9^{11}	14, 27, 32
22^{5-28}	13
22^{14-20}	14

I Chronicles
12^{18}	44
$25^{3f.}$	15

II Chronicles
11^{15}	55
15^1	48

Nehemiah
9^{20}	73
9^{30}	48

Job
4^9	41
27^3	39
33^4	39
$34^{14f.}$	39

Psalms
29	40, 50
51^{11}	37
68	50
104^3	51
$104^{29f.}$	39, 43

Isaiah
2^1	6
4^4	41
$6^{1ff.}$	6, 16
7^{11}	36
8^{11}	48
11^1	49
$11^{2, 11}$	40
21^2	6
22^1	6
28^6	41
$28^{10ff.}$	28
$28^{11f.}$	88
30^{10}	17
30^{16}	51
30^{29}	15
31^3	40
32^{15}	43, 79
34^{14}	55
$38^{1ff.}$	17
40^7	41
$41^{23f.}$	25
42^5	39
42^9	25
$43^{9f.}$	25
43^{10}	26
44^3	79
$45^{7f.}$	25
45^{21}	25
$46^{9f.}$	25
48^5	25
$61^{1f.}$	49

Jeremiah		Daniel		Micah	
1^5	6	2	4	1^1	6
15^{17}	40	4	4	2^6	28
20^9	48	7	4	2^7	48
20^{18-22}	48	8	4	3^5	16
23^{16}	17			3^8	40, 48
$23^{18,\,22}$	48	Hosea			
23^{25-32}	5	4^{12}	40	Habakkuk	
27^2	15	5^4	40	2^2	6
27^9	5, 14	9^7	48	3	50
29^8	5				
29^{26}	32	Joel		Zechariah	
Ezekiel		2^{28}	5, 49	1^8	5
$1^{1f.}$	50	$3^{1ff.}$	79	$2^{1f.}$	5
1^4	36			$3^{1f.}$	5
3^{14}	59	Amos		$4^{1ff.}$	5
11^{19}	79	$3^{7f.}$	48	4^6	40
13^{19}	16	$7^{1-3f.}$	16	$6^{1f.}$	5
$36^{26f.}$	79	7^{12}	17	7^{12}	47
36^{29}	79	7^{16}	28	13^4	20
$37^{1ff.}$	40, 41, 43				

Index of Extra-Biblical Passages

I Maccabees
4^{46} 19, 20
9^{27} 20
14^{41} 19, 20

II Maccabees
12^{40} 55

Tobit
3^8 51

Judith
14^6 51
16^4 51

Ecclesiasticus
1^{19} 52
$4^{12f.}$ 53
15^3 52
$24^{26f.}$ 52
$24^{32f.}$ 52
39^6 73
49^{10} 20

Wisdom of Solomon
$1^{5f.}$ 52, 73
7^7 52, 73
7^{16} 52
7^{27} 53
$8^{7f.}$ 52, 53

Wisdom of Solomon (cont.)
$10^{1f.}$ 52
$11^{1f.}$ 52
12^2 52

I Enoch
$15^{9f.}$ 73
19^1 72
$40^{1f.}$ 28
46^3 19
61^{11} 73
62^2 74
71^{11} 28

Test. Reuben
3^4 73
3^5 73

Test. Simeon
3^1 73
4^7 73

Test. Levi
2^3 73
8^{15} 19
18^7 73

Test. Judah
13^3 73
16^1 73
20^{1-5} 74

Test. Daniel
1^6 73

Sib. Oracles
III.781   19

Asc. Isaiah
8^{17} 28

Apoc. Abram
$17^{1f.}$ 28

II Esdras
$4^{1ff.}$ 6
$5^{21ff.}$ 6
6^{34} 6
$6^{35ff.}$ 6
9^{25} 6
$9^{26ff.}$ 7
$11^{1f.}$ 7
$13^{1ff.}$ 7
$14^{1ff.}$ 7

Manual of Discipline (Dead Sea Scrolls)
$3^{17f.}$ 74
4^{2-8} 74
4^{9-14} 74
$4^{25f.}$ 75

Index of New Testament Passages

Matthew

Passage	Page
1^{18}	67
1^{20}	7, 67
2^{13}	7
4^{24}	71
5^{48}	137
8^{11}	25, 26
$9^{32f.}$	71
9^{34}	70
10^{1}	72
$10^{7ff.}$	25
10^{20}	58, 60
10^{25}	11
11^{18}	70
12^{22}	71
12^{24}	70
12^{28}	67
12^{31}	60
15^{22-8}	71
16^{18}	25
$17^{1ff.}$	7
17^{9}	7
17^{25}	24
21^{11}	20
21^{37}	25
21^{46}	20
$23^{29ff.}$	21, 25
24^{2}	25
26^{3}	25, 26
26^{12}	25
26^{21}	25
26^{64}	26
28^{19}	60

Mark

Passage	Page
$1^{8f.}$	60
1^{10}	67
$1^{12f.}$	67
1^{32}	71
1^{34}	71
1^{39}	71
$3^{11f.}$	67, 71
3^{22}	69
3^{29}	60
5^{30}	24
6^{15}	20
8^{31}	24
$9^{2f.}$	7
9^{33}	24
12^{9}	25
12^{16}	60
14^{30}	25

Luke

Passage	Page
1^{15}	60
1^{35}	60
1^{41}	20, 60
1^{67}	20, 60
$2^{25f.}$	20, 60
$3^{21f.}$	24
3^{22}	67
$4^{1f.}$	60, 67
$4^{14f.}$	60
4^{18}	49, 60
4^{34}	71
4^{41}	71
6^{18}	71
7^{16}	20
7^{21}	71
7^{39}	24
$8^{27ff.}$	71
8^{31}	71
9^{28}	7, 24
10^{21}	60, 61
11^{13}	60, 79, 139
11^{14}	70, 71
11^{20}	72
12^{11}	67
12^{12}	58
$13^{28f.}$	25
13^{33}	21
$17^{1f.}$	26
19^{27}	25
22^{43}	24
24^{19}	20
24^{49}	25, 26, 57, 60, 79, 96

John

Passage	Page
$1^{32f.}$	67
1^{37}	96
2^{25}	24
$3^{5f.}$	62, 67
3^{8}	67
3^{14}	26
3^{34}	62
4^{18}	24
4^{19}	20
4^{24}	62
6^{14}	20
6^{70}	25
$7^{38f.}$	62, 67
7^{40}	20, 21
8^{48}	26
9^{17}	21
11^{6}	24
11^{11}	24
11^{14}	24
12^{22}	26
13^{19}	25
$14^{1f.}$	62, 122
14^{7}	139
14^{16}	79
14^{29}	25
15^{16}	36
15^{26}	79
16^{1}	62
$16^{2ff.}$	25, 26
$17^{20ff.}$	137
18^{27}	26
20^{22}	62
20^{27}	24
21^{18}	25, 26
21^{22}	26
22^{1}	25

Acts

Passage	Page
$1^{4f.}$	57, 96
1^{5}	68
1^{8}	57
1^{16}	67
$2^{1ff.}$	50, 79, 84, 89, 96
$2^{4f.}$	58, 68, 139
2^{6}	84
2^{7}	90
2^{12}	84, 90
2^{13}	84
2^{14}	84
$2^{22ff.}$	95
2^{33}	67
2^{38}	67
4^{8}	58, 65, 68
4^{13}	65
4^{29}	65
4^{31}	30, 65, 68, 96, 139
4^{32}	65
5^{1}	22
5^{29}	65
5^{32}	67
$5^{40ff.}$	65
6^{3}	68, 139
6^{5}	68, 139
6^{10}	58, 65, 67
$7^{54f.}$	8
$7^{55f.}$	65, 68, 139
$8^{1f.}$	96
8^{5}	8
8^{26}	8, 71
8^{39}	40, 59
$9^{1f.}$	96
$9^{4f.}$	59
9^{10}	9
9^{17}	68
9^{31}	67, 139
$10^{1f.}$	59, 96
10^{11}	127

Acts (cont.)

10^{19}	67
10^{28}	22
10^{38}	67, 72, 139
$10^{44f.}$	30, 67
10^{46}	58, 84, 93
10^{47}	67
11^{12}	67
$11^{15f.}$	67
11^{17}	68
11^{24}	139
$11^{27f.}$	21, 59, 113, 126
12^{1}	21, 126
$12^{7f.}$	9
13^{1}	114
$13^{2ff.}$	22, 67
13^{4}	9, 67
13^{9}	58, 68
15^{8}	67
15^{28}	67
$15^{32f.}$	15, 21, 22, 114
$16^{6f.}$	67
$16^{7f.}$	9, 71
16^{9}	127
$16^{16f.}$	23, 72
17^{6}	139
18^{9}	9
$19^{1ff.}$	96
19^{6}	30, 32, 58, 84, 93
$19^{11f.}$	72
19^{12}	100
20^{23}	59, 67
20^{28}	67
21^{4}	59, 67
21^{9}	23
21^{10}	15, 21, 59, 114
21^{11}	67, 126
22^{6}	8
$22^{17f.}$	127
26^{13}	8
$27^{23f.}$	9
27^{23}	127
28^{25}	67

Romans

5^{5}	68
7	75
8^{1-17}	62
8^{9}	62, 63
8^{15-16}	68
$8^{26f.}$	62, 110
12^{6}	21

Romans (cont.)

15^{13}	62
15^{16}	62

I Corinthians

2^{4}	68
2^{10-14}	68
6^{19}	68
7^{40}	126
11^{5}	21, 113
12	126
12^{1}	101
12^{4-11}	68
12^{6}	113
12^{10}	70
12^{14}	84
$12^{18f.}$	110
$12^{28f.}$	22, 23, 114
13^{1}	101
13^{8}	23
14^{2-25}	31
$14^{5, 24}$	21
14^{6}	22
14^{13}	110
$14^{29ff.}$	21, 127
14^{32-3}	21
15^{8}	8

II Corinthians

1	22
4^{6}	8
$6^{4f.}$	68
9^{8-9}	8
$12^{1f.}$	59

Galatians

$2^{11ff.}$	22
3^{2}	62
$4^{4f.}$	94
5^{16-25}	68
$5^{22f.}$	46, 53, 62
$5^{23f.}$	62

Ephesians

1^{13}	62
2^{5}	114
2^{18}	62
2^{20}	114, 126
3^{16}	62
4^{3}	62
4^{11}	23, 114
4^{28-31}	68

Ephesians (cont.)

4^{30}	62
5^{18}	30
6^{12}	76

Philippians

1^{19}	68
2^{1}	62
$3^{7f.}$	8

Colossians

3^{16}	30

I Thessalonians

4^{8}	68
$5^{19f.}$	114, 127
5^{19-20}	30
5^{23}	137

Hebrews

2^{4}	69
6^{4}	69

II Peter

1^{21}	69

I John

3^{24}	69
4^{5}	69
4^{13}	69
$5^{7f.}$	69

Revelation

1^{10}	59
2^{1}	59
2^{7}	59, 69
2^{8}	59
2^{11}	59, 69
2^{12}	59
2^{17}	59, 69
2^{29}	69
3^{6}	59, 69
3^{13}	59, 69
3^{22}	59, 69
10^{7}	114
11^{18}	114
14^{13}	59, 69
16^{16}	114
18^{20}	114
18^{24}	114
19^{10}	69
22^{17}	69
22^{18}	59

Index of Names

Allen, A. V. G., 125

Barrett, C. K., 26
Bettenson, H., 119
Beyer, H. W., 81, 84, 85
Borchert, O., 26
Bourne, H., 132
Bousset, W., 19
Box, G. H., 19
Brownlee, W. H., 74
Brueys, 102
Bushnell, H., 130
Butterfield, H., 75
Butterworth, G. W., 70

Carrington, P., 99
Casson, S., 35
Celsus, 102
Chadwick, S., 137
Clement of Alexandria, 102
Curtis, O. A., 136

Davenport, F. M., 130
Davidson, A. B., 15
Davidson, W. T., 97
Denney, J., 95
De Soyres, 118
Dimond, S. G., 130, 131
Dodd, C. H., 99
Duhm, H., 55
Dupont-Sommer, A., 74

Eusebius, 116, 121, 124

Findlay, J. A., 92
Flew, R. N., 65
Foakes Jackson and Kirsopp Lake, 54, 86–9
Fox, G., 130

Gray, G. B., 36
Grierson, C. T. P., 26
Guillaume, A., 14, 47
Gwatkin, H. M., 116

Hanna, W., 132, 133, 134
Harnack, A. von, 123, 124
Hopwood, P. G. S., 29, 54, 70, 71–3, 75, 98, 130
Humphries, A. L., 50, 51, 54, 126, 127, 132

Ignatius, 22
Inge, W. R., 47
Irenæus, 101, 114
Irving, 133

James, W., 129
Janet, P., 11
Jones, R. M., 11, 117
Justin Martyr, 114

Karsten, R., 3
Knight, H., 18

Langton, E., 3, 37, 55, 70
Lehmann, E., 3
Lévy-Bruhl, L., 3
Liddell and Scott, 23
Lietzmann, H., 101, 102
Lods, A., 14, 17, 19, 48
Lofthouse, W. F., 18

Macdonald, A. J., 52, 53, 66
Mackenzie, D., 136
Major, Manson, and Wright, 8, 20
Manson, T. W., 27, 56, 103, 104, 105, 106, 137
Marshall, W., 138
Meyer, E., 56, 100
Michaëlis, W., 85–6
Middleton, T. F., 69
Montanus, 115
Montgomery, A., 55
Moore, G. F., 47, 53

Oesterley, W. O. E., 72
Oesterreich, T. K., 56, 102
Origen, 103, 114
Otto, R., 53, 126

Philo, 87, 101
Plato, 23, 102
Pratt, J. B., 130

Rattenbury, J. E., 138
Rees, T., 58
Reitzenstein, R., 101
Robinson, H. W., 36, 38–9
Robinson, T. H., 16, 17

Sangster, W. E., 139
Schmidt, W., 102
Scott, C. A. Anderson, 75, 137
Scott, E. F., 45, 61, 63, 64, 82, 89, 94, 108–11
Scougal, H., 138

Selwyn, E. G., 99
Smith, R., 55
Snaith, N. H., 39, 40–1, 43, 48, 50
Stewart, J. S., 75, 76, 96
Strack and Billerbeck, 56, 81, 88
Swete, H. B., 51, 60, 69, 95, 96, 123–5
Synge, F. C., 108

Taylor, V., 61, 65
Tertullian, 116, 119, 123
Thayer-Grimm, 23, 72
Thomas, W. K. G., 49, 97
Tyerman, L., 131

Volz, P., 28, 45, 103

Walker, D., 92
Walker, T., 18
Wardle, W. L., 15, 17
Weinel, H., 21, 22, 86, 102, 124
Weiss, J., 8
Wendland, H. D., 100, 101
Wesley, J., 130–1, 138
Whale, J., 139
Winstanley, E. W., 57
Wood, I. F., 57

Index of Subjects

Abraham, 1, 5
Ahab, 15
Amos, 15–17
Ascension, 29
Asia Minor, 101–3

Baal, 14 f.
Bath Qōl, see Divine Voice

Catechism, primitive form, 99
Cephas Party, 107 f.; Paul and, 105–11
Corinthian Church, 21, 98 ff.

Daniel, 4
Dead Sea Scrolls, 74
Demons, 55 f., 70 f.; Christ and, 72; Kingdom of, 75; Mastery of, 72; names of, 55 f.; possession by, 71 f., 75
Divine Voice, 7, 53, 87 f.
Dreams, interpretation of, 4; Jesus and, 7; Paul and, 9; primitive man and, 1; prophets and, 5, 6

Ecstasy, among early Methodists, 130 ff.; among Quakers, 130–2; and Paul, 30, 32, 48; in Egypt, 14; Isaiah and, 28; Montanists and, 119 ff.; *nebi'im* and, 27; of Jesus, of prophets, 13 ff., 16, 20, 31; produced artificially, 13 f., 47 f.; psychologists and, 35
Elijah, 16, 45
Elisha, 16
Evil Spirits, *see* Spirit *and* Demons
Ezekiel, 17, 18
Ezra, 6

Gideon, 4
Glossolalia, and Cephas Party, 107 f.; as foreign languages, 82–93; at Corinth, 98 f.; at Pentecost, 29 f.; in Apocrypha, 28; in Asia Minor, 101–3; in Montanism, 119; in Old Testament, 27 f.; later evidences, 92, 129–34; Paul and, 105–11

Healing, 83, 132
Holiness, *see also* Perfection *and* Spirit
Hosea, 17

Ignatius, 22
Irenæus, 22
Irving, 132
Isaiah, 17, 28, 39

Jacob, 3 f.
Jeremiah, 16 f., 39
Jerusalem, fall of, 17 f.
Jesus, and the Spirit, 60–2; as prophet, 20 f., 24–6; baptism, 7; birth, 7 f.; divine voice, 7; Transfiguration, 7
John Hyrcanus, 19, 53
Josephus, 19

Law, 18, 36, *see also* Torah

Messianic Age, 6 f., 9 f., 49
Micaiah, 15 f.
Montanism, authorities and, 116 f.; ecstasy in, 119 ff.; growth of, 23, 115 f.; Spirit doctrine and, 119–24, tenets of, 118 ff.; Tertullian and, 116; truth and error of, 125 f.
Moses, 11 f., 45, 88
Mysticism, 47

Nathan, 16
Nebuchadrezzar, 4
Nephesh, see Spirit

Paul, and glossolalia, 109–12; and prophecy, 31 f.; and Spirit, 62–6; at Ephesus, 30; visions of, 8, 9
Pentecost, and Ascension, 29; explanation of, 82 f.; Hebrew parallels, 80 ff., 87 ff.; Jewish readings for day of, 50; Methodism and, 130, 131, 137–8; modern parallels, 91 ff.; phenomena of, 79, 98; significance of, 95 ff., *see also* Glossolalia
Perfection, 65, 135–40
Prophecy, and Greeks, 23; as preaching, 126 f.; decline of, 18, 53 f.; fall of Jerusalem and, 17 f.; in primitive church, 21 ff., 126 f.; John Baptist and, 20; Montanism and, 121; Paul and, 21 f., 31 f.; revival of, 19; women and, 14, 21
Prophets, band of, 13, 15; clairvoyance of, 12 f.; ecstasy of, 13 ff., 16, 20, 31, 47; false, 15 f., 17 f.; function of, 18; Jesus as, 20 f., 24 f., *see* Prophecy; literary, 15–18; *nabi'*, 12 ff.; New Testament, 18–24, 113 f.; priest and, 18; symbolism and, 15 f.

Quakers, 132

Ruach, 40–2, *see also* Spirit

INDEX OF SUBJECTS

Samuel, 12 f.
Saul, dreams of, 4 f.; ecstasy of, 12–14
Solomon, 4
Spirit, and character, 135; and holiness, 138; and perfection, 65, 137 f.; and New Order, 135 f., 139 f.; and scriptures, 53; and Wisdom, 51 f.; as agent and endowment, 66–9; as breath, 38; as life, 39; as power, 40, 44 f., 75; fruits of, 46, 62 f.; function of, 64 f.; Hebrew interpretation, 35 f.; in early church, 57 ff., 96; in non-canonical writings, 51 ff., 74; indwelling, 139; Jesus and, 60 f., 62; *nephesh*, 38 f.; of God, 50; prophets' experience of, 48 f.; *ruach*, 44; the break-through of God, 36; Wesley's teaching, 138; *see also* Demons
Stephen, 8

Tertullian, 22, 116 ff.
Theophany, 36
Tongues, *see* Glossolalia
Torah, 18, 80 f., 88

Vision, *see* Dreams
Voice from heaven, *see* Divine Voice

Wesley, John, 130, 131, 137, 138

Zechariah, 17